Great New England Churches

65 Houses of Worship that Changed our Lives

GREAT NEW ENGLAND CHURCHES

65 Houses of Worship that Changed our Lives

Robert Mutrux, A.I.A.

The Globe Pequot Press

Chester, Connecticut 06412

To Lynne

How to enjoy this book

This book has no particular beginning nor ending. Open it wherever you like and go wherever your travel plan, your curiosity, or your intuition may lead you.

The churches are grouped chronologically within their respective states, and the states are organized by a particular whim of the publisher in the following order: Massachusetts, Vermont, New Hampshire, Maine, Rhode Island, and Connecticut. Each essay is, at best, little more than a visual and factual introduction to its subject. But it may inspire the reader to search out and discover the wealth of facts and legends that, in each case, merit at least a full volume.

If the church is on the beaten path, pause and assess in relation to its context. If not, seek it out, and try to ascertain why the march of progress has passed it by. Study its profile, its mass, its details, and try to analyze why a structure erected three centuries ago may match, in line and proportion and message, the forms offered by today's prestigious designers.

If possible go inside and sit in the rear for a moment of meditation and contemplation. And ask yourself if, for all their apparent differences, there is not some powerful unseen thread that unites not only every church that was ever built, but each one of us as well, in a way that all of the world's science can neither explain nor undo.

And you will have enjoyed one of the great thrills that life and travel and imagination can afford. Indeed, you may even savour all these things without ever leaving your favorite armchair. If you do, I will have succeeded far beyond my wildest hopes.

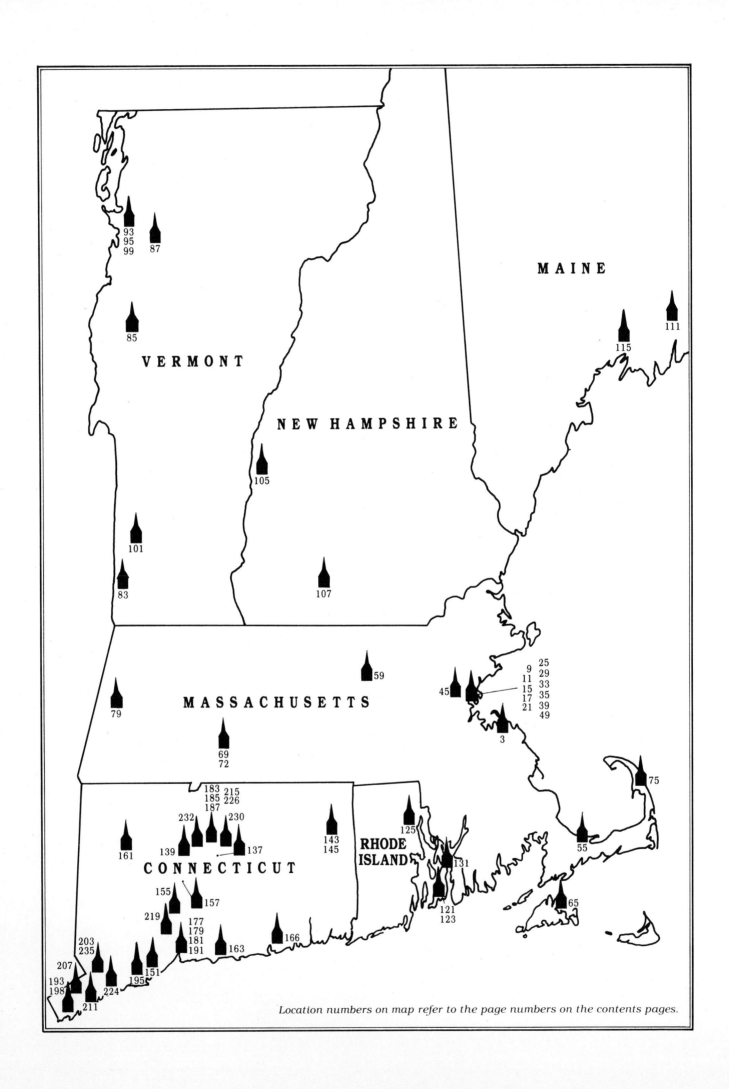

MAINE

VERMONT

93
95
99   87

85

NEW HAMPSHIRE

105

101

83   107

MASSACHUSETTS

59

                                          25
                                    9   29
45   11   33
                                   15   35
                                   17   39
                                   21   49
                              3

79

69
72   75

183   215
185   226
187

232   230   125
161   139   137   143
                                       145   55
CONNECTICUT   RHODE
                         ISLAND
                                          131
155
219   157
           177
           179   166   121
203   181 163   123   65
235   191
207
193   195
198   224
      211

Location numbers on map refer to the page numbers on the contents pages.

Contents

Dates listed here indicate year of completion.
Churches are presented chronologically with each state.

Foreword

Henry James, writing of the young Hawthorne, imagined him gazing out upon a landscape of negatives: "No sovereign, no court . . . no country gentlemen, no palaces, no castles, nor manors, nor old country-houses, nor parsonages, nor thatched cottages, nor ivied ruins; no cathedrals, nor abbeys, nor little Norman churches . . ." By the time, in 1879, that James penned these words, rich Americans were aggressively supplying some of the lacks, including that of ivied ruins, but even in Hawthorne's youth ecclesiastical structures of considerable grandeur existed in New England, in positions of the utmost civic centrality. Perhaps the index of the degree of civilization which James found wanting in his native land lies less in the landscape's furniture than in the intensity of satisfaction with which the living population regard their surrounding of visible heritage. With such books as this enthusiastic and knowledgeable guide by Robert Mutrux, an American can now conduct his own tour of cathedrals without crossing the Atlantic – indeed, by staying within the compass of a pleasant day's drive out of Boston.

The settlement of the Massachusetts Bay sprang from church disputes, and the meetinghouse was the pivot of those first theocratic villages. To this day, the white Protestant spire identifies New England on calendars and postcards:

> *On a thousand small town New England greens,*
> *the old white churches hold their air*
> *of sparse, sincere rebellion . . .*

One of the marvels of Mr. Mutrux's selection of sixty-five notable churches is that he has been able to discriminate among so many—so many white-spired Greek-columned structures lending charm and focus to greens and squares from the borders of Canada to the suburbs of New York City. The selection skimps on the typically picturesque and ranges far in search of striking and persuasive examples of modern church design. The descriptions and photographs are vivid enough to create for the reader in his armchair the illusion of a tour, but undoubtedly the fullest use of this book would be as travel companion, its pages laid open like sabbath church portals on the front seat while its precious subjects are approached mile after rolling mile and discovered within their often cluttered and incongruous settings.

As with the stone cathedrals of Western Europe, one may be struck, sadly, by their grand emptiness, an emptiness as yet little relieved, in America, by the shuffle of other tourists. The religious *raison d'être* of handsome churches sometimes persists as a furtive and feeble undercurrent to the architecture, an embarrassing human impurity—in Europe, the guttering votive candle and unshaven sacristan; in America, the tattered bulletin board and wistful pamphlet rack and garish decorations provided by the Sunday School. Many of the churches described within have slipped from one denomination to another; a number sit in neighborhoods that no longer form an adequate parish; some, including one of the most recent, the Michael Pierce Chapel in Lenox, (see page 79), have passed into secular use. All, it seems safe to say, present headaches to their building committees and cost far more to heat than formerly. Joy and aspiration have shaped these churches, but a certain melancholy may fill them. Puritanism faded into Unitarianism and thence into stoic agnosticism; these gallant old shells hold more memories than promises. Robert Lowell, who wrote the lines above, wrote as well:

> *I see His vanishing*
> *emblems, His white spire and flag-*
> *pole sticking out above the fog,*
> *like old white china doorknobs, sad,*
> *slight, useless things to calm the mad.*

Like Mr. Mutrux, I came late to New England. The first regional church of which I had experience was Harvard's Memorial Chapel, that splendid but slightly cold reproduction of the Colonial manner, with its immaculate box pews and huge dark choir screen. Attending, I would sit back on the left-hand side near a small bronze plaque that seemed to me the epitome of New England fair-mindedness; opposite the great wall covered with the names of Harvard alumni killed fighting for the Allies, the plaque gave the names of four German graduates *"qui diversis sub signis pro patria spiritum reddiderunt,"* beneath a transcendent assurance: *"Academia Harvardiana non oblita est filiorum suorum"* – Harvard has not forgotten her sons.

Returning some years later to live north of Boston, I would attend the Congregational church in Ipswich, a handsome, town-dominating example of "carpenter Gothic" exactly contemporaneous with the First Parish Church in Brunswick, Maine (see page 113), and, like it, tipped wooden pinnacles and walled with boards and battens. The interior posed a delicate white-painted heaven of shapely roof trussing; the light came through tall pointed windows of old gray-glass lozenge panes. Some winter mornings, hardly a dozen of us showed up, while the minister shouted across the empty pews and the groaning furnace in the basement sent up odorous warmth through the cast-iron grates and the wind leaned on the crackling panes. I have never felt closer to the bare bones of Christianity than on those bleak and drafty Sunday mornings, with the ghosts of frock-coated worshippers and patient carpenters making up for our sparse attendance. That church is gone; it burned down one stormy June day in 1965; one hundred nineteen years old, it had stood longer than any of its four predecessors on the site and has now been succeeded by a stocky sixth edifice of white brick. Through its hushed and graceful spaces, so different from the colorful and stolid Lutheran interiors of my childhood, I entered into the spiritual life of my adopted region.

Can this life be distinguished, even minutely, from that of other regions? It is tinctured by the Puritan beginnings and the stony soil, the four sharp seasons and the nautical outlook of the indented shore. To Calvinism, Irish Catholicism added its own austerities and wit. Is it too fanciful to imagine a certain stylistic humor that pervades even the great urban barns of Romishness and Anglicanism, the mock-ecclesiastical institutional buildings of Yale, and the perfect little Russian Orthodox church that Igor Sikorsky and some of his employees erected in the worst days of World War Two (see page 195) — a living humor that licenses the creativity of the modern church architects so liberally represented herein? "Live free or die" runs the motto of one of our six states, and there does seem to be an extra tang of the free, of the voluntary, in our chilly, salty local air. The New England spirit does not seek solutions in a crowd; raw light and solitariness are less dreaded than welcomed as enhancers of our essential selves. And our churches, classically, tend to seek through their forms, so restrainedly adorned, their essence as houses for the inner light.

John Updike
Georgetown, Massachusetts

Acknowledgements

My sincere thanks:

To Bob Wilkerson for his suggestion that I write this book;

To all the pastors, historians, and architects who responded to my
   requests for information;

To my fellow architect, Rocco Fabrizio, for his superb sketches;

To all the photographers who provided photos without which this work
   would have been totally lacking in clarity and meaning;

To my daughter Robin, for her expert editorial advice;

And to Babby Agnew and Egea Logan for their patient and thorough
   secretarial assistance.

Introduction

As far back as I can remember, churches have fascinated me. My introduction to this special and persistent type of building was a tiny Irvingite chapel on the outskirts of St. Louis. My parents brought their twelve children there on the first Sunday of each month to participate in the Catholic-Apostolic service. It was a grey wooden structure with varnished wood inside; it was similar in proportion to the New England meetinghouse but it had pointed arches and the pale yellow leaded-glass windows. The chapel held about sixty persons, including the Boehmes, the Halbergs, the Lundblads, the Lemps, and the Knudsens who, like ourselves, had twelve children. I clearly remember Milton Boehme who, after stoking the pot-bellied stove near the entrance, would proceed to the front to perform as required on the foot-pedaled harmonium. The service was hardly exciting, except when Mr. Wood, the Prophet, would suddenly, without warning, justify his title in a thundering bass voice.

On the other three Sundays, we attended Ascension Episcopal Church in the city itself. This structure was red brick pseudo-Tudor Gothic, with no pretensions, but quite grand by our standards. Two of my eight brothers and I sang in the choir, which was led by the organist, Ray Douglas. Under his inspired direction, we sang all those grand hymns and chanted the psalms; we also sang the anthems, cantatas, the oratorios which, in those far-off days, were an integral part of the Episcopal service. And I was completely carried away, not so much by the liturgy as by the way in which Ray Douglas filled the space with his brilliant unrelentingly fortissimo improvisations on the organ.

Of course we did all the things that choir boys usually do. But above all, we loved the church, the music, the social contacts, and we began to sense the special mystique that is the result of the sounds, the colors, the quiet and the drama of the service and the awe-inspiring interior, all of which combine to create an atmosphere that is found in no other type of structure.

This period was followed by the most glorious year of my life. My father took his whole family – with two automobiles – to his native

Switzerland. We lived in Renens, near Lausanne, for a year, during which we went to school, we climbed mountains, we skied, and we went regularly to the Catholic-Apostolic church. But most important, we saw all of Europe. We saw the museums, the palaces, all the great cities of Europe. And in Paris, London, Rome, Seville, Cologne, we visited all the great churches that line the squares and boulevards of the western world. And I have been hopelessly hooked on churches ever since.

Five years of architectural school and a bout with the Depression were followed by the World's Fair and the World War, and then twenty-five years as a practicing architect in Connecticut. At present I am teaching the appreciation of architecture. Churches fascinate me as much as they did that year at the age of sixteen, when I first saw Notre Dame de Chartres, Santa Maria del Fiore, St. Peter's and St. Paul's and Cologne. And I still wonder why.

Is it because of their distinctive architectural facades, the interior arrangement of the voids and solids and light? Many railroad stations and libraries and shopping malls possess these same qualities.

Is it because of the decoration, the frescoes, the mosaics? Our museums have better frescoes and mosaics and even stained-glass than most churches.

Is it because of the music, the reverberation of the sound of the organ as it invades the interior of the church, and penetrates the recesses of your imagination and memory? The concert halls do as well, and the stereo far better.

Why do we all find ourselves seized by a special sensation when we enter a church, one that we do not sense in any other type of building? Perhaps there is no fully satisfying explanation. But I have my own theory, for whatever it may be worth.

The church differs from all other buildings because in many ways it is like a book. The doors of a church open like those of a book, even though they are hinged at the sides, while those of a book are hinged together at the middle. Both the church and a book are enclosures. A book encloses ideas, framed in letters and words and chapters on paper pages. A church encloses certain human activities, within a frame made of bricks and beams and walls and roof.

Both are invitations, of a special sort. The book is an invitation to the world of ideas, as wide and broad as the reader's imagination. And the church, unlike any other building, is an invitation to the world of the spirit, whose scope is not measured by the builder's plan, but by the aims and desires and dreams of its users.

The invitation of the church, though as real as it is infinite, cannot be captured within mere words or phrases or dimensions. It is elusive, challenging, indescribable, indefinable, infinite and eternal. And the sensation is the same in the modest wooden meetinghouse as it is in the cathedral.

This book does not attempt to analyze the peculiar fascination of the church building. It is written simply to bring attention to certain variations of that timeless theme as they appear in the New England states, covering all styles, denominations, and architectural periods.

The selection of churches is limited to the better-known examples, including a few discoveries of my own. The list is not intended to be final or exclusive; I shall be criticized as much for what I have included as for what I have omitted. My intention is mainly to arouse interest in an aspect of human creativity in the New England states that is forever and everywhere present, always stimulating, and highly revealing.

This presentation may invite the readers to see what fragment of the church's message may be revealed to them, and help them at the same time to enjoy a small but important portion of our nation's architecture and history.

Robert H. Mutrux, AIA

The Boston Churches

Boston possesses a respect for human scale that is rare among large population centers. This is an indefinable yet easily recognizable element that is characterized by oases of relative quiet, by the occasional absence of the audio-visual demands of commerce and politics, and the acknowledgement of nature itself as a necessary part of our day-to-day existence.

Boston, to me, resembles the typical medieval city. The crooked (and maddeningly) one-way streets, bursting with surprises at every turn and the paved squares, blissfully devoid of automobile traffic, are an undeniable delight to the visitor and are qualities that seem to be fully enjoyed by the city's residents.

Surprises and open space are found only sporadically in London and Paris, seldom in Rome, and almost never in Washington, D.C. In Boston, though moments of architectural grandeur exist in ample number, islands of intimacy and repose are always only a few blocks distant. And the center of visual interest, as in every medieval city, is almost invariably a house of worship.

By a pleasant coincidence, Boston's churches fall into a pattern that becomes the nation's first great musical center. While New Haven, Hartford and Burlington each boast a triad of churches, Boston, to continue the musical analogy, has an important solo, a duet, a trio, a quartet and many other manifestations of "frozen music," to use Goethe's well-known phrase.

Indeed, in a city with well over 500 houses of worship, one could include enough important edifices to make up several symphonies, each with full chorus.

Old Ship Meetinghouse, Unitarian; Hingham, Massachusetts

"Let the work of our fathers stand."

Old Ship Meetinghouse, Unitarian
107 Main Street, Hingham, Massachusetts 02043

Completed on January 8, 1682   **Charles Stockbridge, builder**

The town of Hingham is only a few miles off the expressway south from Boston to Cape Cod, and the detour will be richly rewarding. Its principal attraction, the Unitarian Church, is a veritable treasure chest of history, architecture, religion and human psychology.

The "Old Ship Meetinghouse" is New England's oldest church in continuous use. It is also the oldest remaining meetinghouse and the oldest frame house of worship in America (St. Luke's Episcopal Church in Smithfield, Virginia built in 1632, is in brick, as is Williamsburg's Bruton Parish Church, dated 1682).

The story of the discovery and restoration of Hingham's masterpiece is a fascinating tale of coincidence and good fortune. It was erected in 1681; in 1731 a plaster ceiling (an obvious forerunner of today's energy-saving solutions) was installed below the roof trusses to conserve heat. In 1791 sixty members of the church, unmindful of the treasure overhead, voted to tear down the meetinghouse and replace it with a more "contemporary" structure. A minority of twenty-eight, however, though equally ignorant of the real worth of the building, was able to overrule them and convinced them to "let the work of their fathers stand."

Then 139 years later, in 1930, Edgar Walker, a Boston architect with a genius for restoration, climbed into the attic and discovered the wealth of architecture that had been concealed and preserved for two centuries.

The scene in which Walker first perceived the hand-hewn wood framing can be compared to that of Tom Sawyer when he first spied the horde of gold in the cave. To the dedicated architectural historian, the feeling must have been not unlike that aroused by archeologist Howard Carter's first view of the treasures of Tutankhamen. Walker was "the right man in the right place" to preserve one of the most significant examples of Colonial religious architecture and further enrich the pageant of American architecture as a whole.

One has only to compare the exposed wood trusses of the Old Ship Church in Hingham today with the acres of ornamental plaster ceilings that followed to understand why Walker's discovery was so important.

The exterior of the Old Ship Meetinghouse is not overly impressive because it is perched rather uncomfortably on a high knoll that has been truncated, vertically and mercilessly, to allow for unimpeded automobile traffic. The building does not command attention like its Unitarian colleague in Lancaster, whose building committee spent many well-documented hours selecting the best site solely for "the view."

And yet the Old Ship Church represents, for posterity, the total architectural expression of the Puritan ethic. It is the individual and the full community represented in a visual symbol. According to William Pierson, the historian, the church was "first of all a house of worship, but it concerned itself in the social and economic affairs of the community." The building remained a special tribute to that healthy, happy symbiosis of Church and State until the last town meeting held there in 1827.

In its present form, the Meetinghouse is a rectangular box, 55' by 73', with a pitched roof surmounted by a modest cupola of a later date. The proportions are not unpleasant. Gladys Stark, in the official brochure, refers to it as " . . . a quaint old lady cherishing a bygone bonnet plus a fancied intermediate fashion or two."

It exemplifies all those hundreds of "meetinghouses" that once covered New England like Romanesque chronicler Raoul Glaber's "blanket of snow," but which were all replaced in the early 1800s by the present Federal and Greek Revival "churches." In this fortunate case, the contemporary taste of the majority did not prevail.

The interior is a revelation. The space is basically a rectangle populated with box pews under spacious yet simple galleries on three sides. It is crowned, however, by one of the most beautiful exposed trussed roofs in all of America. The breathtaking effect of the interior has often been compared to the famous circular Shaker barn in Hancock, Massachusetts, whose radiating rafters create the effect of Gothic vaulting.

Here the sturdy forms and the ingenious structural pattern of the great timber trusses are awe-inspiring. In building what was undoubtedly intended as a straightforward barn structure, the Puritans attempted, in the best tradition, to reject the self-conscious "church-like" effect of the Anglican edifice. They sought, above all, to eschew any semblance of ostentation in their work. And yet the result of their effort was a paradigm of self-expression. Without intending to do so, they created a significant work of art.

The roof construction, though self-effacing in its anonymity, is highly expressive in its result. It is the apothesis of individual and community effort. In this respect, the ceiling reflects the same mystique that surrounds the construction of the cathedrals of the Middle Ages. And the result is a space filled, day and night, with the presences of all those who once populated it with their faith and their work, just like their medieval counterparts.

The innumerable workmen are there, their calloused handprints on the 45-foot hand-adzed tie-beams as well as on the wooden pegs, impregnated with sweat, that hold the beams captive. And there is the signa-

Edgar Walker was immediately struck by the individuality of the roof construction, which suggests the ribs of a ship's hull.

ture of the master craftsman (perhaps a ship's carpenter) who, in a moment of unquestionably divine inspiration, ordered the top braces to be curved rather than straight. This step, made for no conceivable structural purpose, must have been the result of an unconscious esthetic impulse. In an instant of self-expression, human pride (anathema to the self-righteous Puritan) imposed itself on the generations that followed and gave the entire structure its individuality.

It is this human quality, this moment of special devotion, that overrode the strictly Puritan ethic and one that cannot honestly be separated from individual vanity. And it is this mystical element without which history would be totally devoid of its heritage of great buildings.

The cost of construction of the Old Ship Meetinghouse is recorded as

430 pounds sterling. This sum was raised by assessing the parishioners, numbering 335, according to their means. Edward Sinnott, dean of meetinghouse historians, records that Daniel Cushing paid fifteen pounds, one shilling and sixpence, while Joseph Jones paid in only five shillings and John Beale, "an ancient Father in Israel," contributed nothing save, of course, the dignity of his presence and his years.

————————

Services: Sunday, 10:30 a.m.
Seating Capacity: 400
Open to visitors: July and August, 12 to 5 p.m. Otherwise by appointment.
Telephone: (617) 749-1679
Construction Cost: 430 pounds sterling
How to get there: Take Route 3, then Route 3A south from Boston to Hingham and ask for Hingham Square. First Parish Office is at 107 Main Street. The Meetinghouse is at 90 Main Street.

Architect:**Charles Stockbridge's** biography not available.

North End Duet

Christ Church Episcopal

Saint Stephen's Roman Catholic Church

Christ Church Episcopal; Boston, Massachusetts

Christ Church Episcopal

(Originally Old North Church)
193 Salem Street, Boston, Massachusetts 02113

Completed on December 29, 1723   **William Price, designer**

This trim brick edifice appears to be serenely oblivious to the noisy secular activities of the Italian communities crowded about its base. The church lacks only the piazza or square with which, in any other Mediterranean ambience, it would surely have been dignified.

Christ Church is possibly, even probably, the "Old North Church" immortalized in Longfellow's epic poem; indeed, its association with Paul Revere, among other things, seems to make any questions of historic validity seem pedantic and ungallant.

It was designed by William Price, gentleman-amateur, who, through his travels and his activities as a bookseller, must have been acquainted with the architecture of Christopher Wren. The basic plan is unusual because the entrance is on the narrow side, under the tower, and not on one of the long sides. Trinity Episcopal Church in Newport, though in wood, is similar in plan and in the detail of the spire.

The tower that housed the two famous lanterns was destroyed by a hurricane in 1804 and replaced under the direction of Charles Bulfinch. Another hurricane again destroyed that tower in 1954, but the weathervane, made by one Shem Drowne, survived each tempest and is back in place. Annually, on April 18, the "Hanging of the Lanterns" (by Paul Revere's associates) is celebrated. Three lanterns are hung, the third to celebrate a third century of freedom, liberty and peace.

Christ Church is the repository of the famous "Vinegar Bible," donated to the parish by George II in 1733. The Bible was so named (and became a $100,000 collector's item) because of the misspelling in the phrase "Parable of the Vineyard."

Services: Sunday, 9:30 and 11 a.m., 4 p.m.   **Telephone:** (617) 523-6676
Seating Capacity: 500   **Construction Cost:** Unknown.
Open to visitors: 9 a.m. to 5 p.m. daily.
How to get there: Ask for Boston's "North End," then ask for Salem Street and the Paul Revere Mall.

Designer: **Price, William,** print-seller. Born in England, no dates available.

Saint Stephen's Roman Catholic Church; Boston, Massachusetts

St. Stephen's Roman Catholic Church

(Originally New North Congregational Church)
401 Hanover Street, Boston, Massachusetts 02109

Completed in 1804   **Charles Bulfinch, architect**

St. Stephen's Church is Bulfinch's only remaining church in the Boston area. By itself, the church is of minor architectural importance. But it is a vital element in a triumph in urban design, because it is intimately associated with Christ Church Episcopal on the Paul Revere Mall, a lovely, tree-lined surprise that both separates and connects the two structures.

They are mutually removed, to be sure, by certain liturgical road-blocks; they are united, however, under the name of Bulfinch, who completed the New North Church in 1804, the same year that he repaired the spire on Old North, known today as Christ Church Episcopal.

In 1814, New North became Second Unitarian. Shortly thereafter, the vacuum created by the westward shift of the city's Protestant population was filled by the influx of Italian-born immigrants. The Roman Catholic Archdiocese purchased the church and renamed it St. Stephen's Roman Catholic Church in 1862.

The design is distinctively Bulfinch in that it eliminated the traditional Congregational spire and the succession of telescoping sections in favor of a simple dome. The latter is the only element that is reflected, ten years later, in Bulfinch's design for Lancaster's famous Unitarian Church (see page 59). However, the general effect of the facade is reflected in Boston's "West Church," by Asher Benjamin (see page 26), whom Bulfinch strongly influenced.

St. Stephen's is a graceful and refreshing addition to Boston's richly-varied religious scene. To me, its interior is marred by the startling incongruity of the huge gold-domed tabernacle that proclaims the church's denominational identity in what one unconsciously still considers to be a Protestant preserve. This detail, however, is only a minor note of discord in the chorus of universal human verities that brought so many divergent creeds and their respective architectural images to Boston's fertile and receptive shores.

Services: Daily, 7:30 a.m.; Saturday, 5:30 p.m.; Sunday, 7:30, 9:30, 11:30 a.m.

Seating Capacity: 700
Open to visitors: 9 a.m. to 5 p.m. daily.
Telephone: (617) 523-1230
Construction Cost: Unknown.
How to get there: Take the Massachusetts Turnpike extension to Atlantic Avenue. Then take Commercial Street to Hanover Street. The church faces the Paul Revere Mall, which connects it to the Old North Church.

Architect: **Bulfinch, Charles.** 1763-1844. Born in Boston, Massachusetts. Bulfinch was educated at Harvard and traveled extensively in Europe. Works represented: St. Stephen's Church, Boston and First Unitarian Church, Lancaster, Massachusetts (see page 59). Bulfinch is best known for the design of Boston's Old State House, Connecticut State House in Hartford, and numerous residences, churches, banks, and other buildings in the Boston area. He was appointed architect of the United States Capitol in 1817.

Old South Meetinghouse

Park Street Congregational Church

King's Chapel

Beacon Hill Quartet

Old West Church

Old South Meetinghouse; Boston, Massachusetts

Old South Meetinghouse
Third Congregational Church

310 Washington Street, Boston, Massachusetts 02108

Completed in April 1730   **Joshua Blanchard, builder**

New England's longest meetinghouse, 96 by 67 feet, is almost identical in area to Providence's eighty-foot square First Baptist church (see page 125). Its 180-foot steeple is five feet shorter than Rhode Island's famous Gibbs-inspired symbol. But it equals Providence's famous church in its close association with the nation's history.

On December 16, 1773, some 7,000 persons assembled in and around Old South prior to their historic march down to Griffin's Wharf to express their indignation over Britain's Stamp Act.

In the winter of 1775, General Burgoyne's troops were stationed near there, and it is recorded that his light cavalry practiced inside its walls. And from the side windows, one can view the site of Benjamin Franklin's birthplace.

Old South is another conspicuous focal point in the city's endless series of pleasant architectural surprises. It appears first at the head of Washington Street, unmistakable among the proliferation of commercial buildings of all sizes and types. Then, if one looks back from Milk Street, its delicate ornamented spire, rising above the unadorned, understated brick tower, is framed in the anonymous metal and glass outlines of a quarter-millennium later.

What an appropriate symbol for the survival of the spirit – if not over the mind and body – at least in a colorful and esthetically balanced coexistence!

Joshua Blanchard, master-builder of Boston, is credited with the construction. Despite the Congregationalist aversion to anything remotely associated with the Church of England, the overall design and proportions may have been influenced by Old North Episcopal Church, completed six years earlier.

Services: None
Seating Capacity: 650
Open to visitors: Winter: 10 a.m. to 4 p.m. daily; Summer: 10 a.m. to 6 p.m. daily.

Telephone: (617) 482-6439

Construction Cost: Unknown.

How to get there: The church is on the Freedom Trail in the downtown business district, at the corner of Washington and Milk Streets.

Architect: **Unknown. Joshua Blanchard's** biography also not available.

The meetinghouse, having weathered its voyage, is transformed from a ship into a stately meetingroom, expressive of security, success, and established cultural values.

16

King's Chapel, Unitarian

64 Beacon Street, Boston, Massachusetts 02108

Completed in August 1753   **Peter Harrison, architect**

A long stone's throw up Tremont St. from Old South Church is an odd-appearing edifice which, despite its name, is not a chapel at all, but an impressive ecclesiastical monument sheathed in solemn grey granite.

I must confess that I find the exterior of King's Chapel rather forbidding, the style anachronistic, and its proportions quite clumsy. The Ionic-columned portico, recalling a section of London's British Museum, seems to presage the Greek Revival of a near century later. The whole composition, crowned by a heavy square base for an unfinished tower, threatens to slide downhill into the Second-Empire Old City Hall.

I have no reservations, however, concerning its interior. It is a masterpiece in proportion, in detail, and in architectural grandeur. The two-story Corinthian columns and the precise Roman detailing form a glorious, harmonious unit that is reflected, but not matched, in two of Hartford's impressive churches (see pages 183 and 185).

King's Chapel is the work of Peter Harrison, the nation's first gentleman-amateur-architect. Sea captain and merchant from Newport, he was among the first to span the gap between the master-carpenter-builder and today's professional architect.

Harrison was approached in 1748 by the rector, Henry Caner, who wrote that "The committee should consider it a Favour if you should oblige them with a draught of a handsome church . . ."

As noted in Andre Mayer's excellent brochure, "Favour" is the right word; there was no question of paying the gentleman for his work (This approach may mystify my colleagues, most of whom are gentlemen as well as architects. The fact that Thomas Jefferson also followed this procedure is unconvincing. Most of them are aware that Jefferson died penniless.)

The term "handsome" is equally revealing. The committee was made up largely of Anglicans "to whom rank, wealth, political power and religion reinforce each other," and they made it clear that their church should reflect these characteristics.

Harrison responded grandly, and at three levels. He designed an edifice which, in its interior, echoed their pretensions; he created a

King's Chapel, Unitarian; Boston, Massachusetts

symbol of worship which distinguished the Anglicans from their Congregational contemporaries, and then firmly affixed his own signature.

His approach was successful in the best sense. You will note, as I finally did, that the four churches in the Beacon Hill Quartet are individually quite distinctive. Old South Church (see page 15) is a Wren-type edifice; Park Street Congregational Church (see page 21) is in the tradition of Gibbs, and Old West Church (see page 25) records the influence of Bulfinch filtered through Asher Benjamin.

In this context, one might call attention to the four buildings on Athens' acropolis which, in a harmonious variety of forms, express a unity of purpose. How hideous, had they all been identical!

Oddly enough, King's Chapel, New England's first Anglican church, became the nation's first Unitarian church in 1785. Apparently there was no great difficulty in accommodating the existing church to a different faith. In 1816 Paul Revere cast the church's two-and-a-half-ton bell and inscribed it "The sweetest bell we ever made." The big church organ maintained the church's position at the center of Boston's musical life for many years. All of this helps, somehow, to justify the persistence of my musical analogy.

Services: Sunday, 11 a.m. to 12 noon; Wednesday, 12:15 to 12:25 p.m.
Seating Capacity: 700

The meetinghouse is no longer a modest and grateful refuge. It has now become a proud procession: a self-flattering acknowledgement of its creator's material accomplishments.

Open to visitors: Tuesday to Saturday, 10 a.m. to 4 p.m.
Telephone: (617) 227-2155
Construction Cost: Unknown.
How to get there: Park in the Undercommon Garage in Boston, and take the free bus to the corner of Tremont and Beacon Streets.

Architect: **Harrison, Peter,** successful merchant and gentleman-architect. 1716-1775. Born in Yorkshire, England. Work represented: King's Chapel, Boston (see page 17) and Touro Synagogue, Newport, Rhode Island. Harrison also designed Christ Church in Cambridge, Massachusetts and several outstanding residences in Newport. New England patriots burned his home, his extensive architectural library and his drawings because of his Tory politics.

Park Street Congregational Church

1 Park Street, Boston, Massachusetts 02108

Completed on January 10, 1809   **Peter Banner, builder, designer**

Henry James once called Park Street Church "the most impressive mass of brick and mortar in America." Coming from one noted for his eloquence, this is faint praise indeed.

The Castel St. Angelo in Rome might be referred to as a "mass of brick and mortar." But Park Street Church in Boston deserves far better. Its main feature is not the body of the church, which is blended into adjacent buildings, but the slender spire that English architect Christopher Wren introduced into his designs to simulate the "fleche," or "arrow," pointing skyward in the Gothic church.

English-born Peter Banner's delicate design pierces the horizon at the northeast corner of Boston Common. It is mounted on the characteristic square brick base, developing into three telescoping octagons and terminating in an attenuated cone. The graceful spire is not matched in all of New England, not even by New Haven's handsome Center Church (see page 179).

Few Gothic churches ever enjoyed a more flattering emplacement, and no church deserved it more. Unfortunately, though this lovely edifice dominates the Common, it does not squarely face the inviting open space. It is oriented, not to the west, in the manner of great cathedrals, but southeast, perhaps to anticipate the surge of oncoming Unitarians. Thus it attains a dynamic rather than a static stance, but its strategy is rudely blocked by the frustrating one way traffic of Tremont Street. (The Unitarian tactic was to engage the same Peter Banner to design their church in Burlington, Vermont (see page 93).

Though the Park Street Church suffers in its rather awkward setting, its silhouette alone is nevertheless overwhelming.

It was in the Park Street Church, according to Edmund Sinnott, architectural chronicler of New England Meetinghouses, that the hymn "America" was first sung publicly. Again, Boston's pervasive music syndrome.

Services: Sunday, 10:30 a.m., 7:30 p.m.

Park Street Congregational Church; Boston, Massachusetts

Open to visitors: Monday to Friday, 9 a.m. to 5 p.m.
Seating Capacity: 1100 to 1200
Telephone: (617) 523-3383
Construction Cost: $40,000
How to get there: The church is at the northeast corner of the Boston Common, at Park and Tremont Streets.

Designer: **Banner, Peter,** house carpenter and master builder. Born and trained in England, no dates available. Work represented: Park Street Church, Boston and Unitarian Church, Burlington, Vermont (see page 93). Banner also designed the Eben Crafts House, Roxbury, Massachusetts.

Old West Church; Boston, Massachusetts

Old West Church

131 Cambridge Street, Boston, Massachusetts 02114

Completed in 1806   **Asher Benjamin, architect**

Fourth in this amorphous group, and least interesting architecturally, is Old West Church. Formerly a United Methodist Church, it is now a branch public library. I am immediately reminded of Dwight Hall at Yale University, designed as a library and transformed into the college chapel. And of St. Basil's Cathedral in Moscow and the Cathedral of the Spilled Blood in Leningrad, both of which are now museums. All this must have some special meaning.

But more important, Old West joins that long list of New England churches and meetinghouses which were made famous by their association with those who, in the garb of the ministry, were far more active in the defense of civil liberty than in the propagation of the faith. Among these were Jonathan Mayhew and Simeon Howard, rectors, who probably saw the British troops turn the original church into firewood in 1775, but neither of whom lived to see the new church completed in 1806. Needless to say, the State today owes much of its current happy symbiosis with the Church to Old West, whose hospitality it enjoyed, presumably free of charge, in our nation's early beginnings.

The church was designed by Asher Benjamin, a native of Greenfield, Massachusetts. He was a great admirer of the work of Charles Bulfinch, and perhaps the principal claim of Old West to architectural importance is its somewhat distant resemblance to Bulfinch's St. Stephen's Church in the North End (see page 11).

Benjamin's name is also linked with that of Ithiel Town in the design of Center Church in New Haven (see page 179), a far more graceful and satisfying project, completed in 1814. In addition, Benjamin was one of the first of many architects who, through their books, established a standard of quality throughout the art of their times. Benjamin's five books, though heavily Gibbsian and Palladian in flavor, "helped mightily," according to the historian Alan Gowans, "to spread the Greek Revival style throughout New England."

Here I am reminded of the atmosphere of two generations ago when we perused, with great ardor, the superb Beaux Arts presentations of D'Espouy and Stuart & Revett, and of the tremendous influence of the books of Frank Lloyd Wright and Le Corbusier on the generation just past.

Whose writings today will be referred to when the architectural history of the current anarchic period is put into print?

———————

Service: Sunday, 11 a.m.
Open to visitors: Monday to Friday, 9 a.m. to 2:30 p.m.
Seating Capacity: 350
Telephone: (617) 227-5088
Construction Cost: Unknown.
How to get there: The church is located between the JFK Building and Massachusetts General Hospital. Take the Government Center "T" and walk west on Cambridge Street.

Architect:**Asher Benjamin,** author. 1771-1845. Born in Greenfield, Massachusetts. Work represented: Designed Old West Church, Boston, Massachusetts. Benjamin also designed several Boston residences. He is best known as author of *The Country Builder's Assistant* and several widely used and influential books on architecture.

First Lutheran Church

Back Bay Trio

First Baptist Church

Church of the Covenant

Church of the Covenant; Boston, Massachusetts

28

Church of the Covenant

67 Newbury and Berkeley Streets, Boston, Massachusetts 02116

Completed in 1867   **Richard M. Upjohn, architect**

"We have one steeple in Boston which to my eyes seems absolutely perfect: that of the Central Congregational Church (today called Church of the Covenant). Its resemblance to the spire of Salisbury (England) has always struck me. One of our best living architects agrees with me as to its similarity. On the other hand, on mentioning this to the late Mr. Richardson, the very distinguished architect, he said to me that he thought it more nearly like that of the Cathedral of Chartres." These are the words of Oliver Wendell Holmes, as quoted in the *Boston Evening Transcript* of May 5, 1934. And their implication has been justly repeated many times since, by authors, jurists, and critics. In my estimation, the Church of the Covenant is a paradigm of the Gothic Revival style, ranking with St. Mary's Church in Stamford (see page 193) and Holy Cross Church in Holyoke (see page 69); both were built a supposedly more sophisticated half-century later.

The 1934 quotation was a dying echo of the educated reaction of an entire century of Revival architecture. Quality since the time of Jefferson was measured by architectural eclecticism, not by intrinsic creativity. Even the gifted and prolific Richardson, who managed to extricate himself from the grip of Neo-Gothic (which had only recently shed the shackles of the Neo-Classic) immersed himself in a style which could only be called a resurrection of the Romanesque.

In Holmes' day, the "giants" of the twentieth century, though acknowledged by the profession itself, had not yet established a firm foothold on the current world of taste and culture.

Fortunately for our ever-changing architectural environment, the quality of workmanship, the depth of inspiration, and the unquestioned sincerity of the century of Revivals established a level of culture that the twentieth century was forced to match before the intelligentsia would grant their own imprimatur.

And in this respect, the ever-changing old Church of the Covenant is a landmark not to be surpassed, an acknowledged religious monument as durable as it is inspiring that rises well above its mundane Twentieth century ambience. It lacks only the park-like setting of Salisbury

Cathedral or the broad parvis of Chartres to make it one of the nation's great monuments.

It was designed by Richard M. Upjohn, son of the architect for New York's Trinity Church on Wall Street (Richard Upjohn, Jr. also designed Hartford's Gothic high-Victorian state capitol).

It rests on 1100 wooden piles; its vaults rise to 60 feet, and its 242-foot spire exceeds Bunker Hill Monument in height by twenty feet.

An outstanding feature of the interior is the breathtaking panorama of "Tiffany" windows, by the firm of Louis Tiffany of New York. By today's standards, this feature alone is sufficient to make this church a national landmark.

It was called "Central Congregational Church" until 1932 when the Congregational community joined with the First Presbyterian Church and recorded this ecumenical event in the church's present name.

———————

Services: Sunday, 11 a.m.

Open to visitors: Tuesday to Saturday, 10 a.m. to 5 p.m.

Seating Capacity: 700

Telephone: (617) 266-7480

Construction Cost: Unknown

How to get there: The church is located in the Back Bay area of Boston, one block off Commonwealth Avenue at Newbury and Berkeley Streets.

Architect: **Upjohn, Richard Mitchell.** 1827-1903. Born in Shaftesbury, England. Son of Richard Upjohn, architect. Upjohn was educated in New York City and trained as an architect in his father's office. He continued in his father's footsteps, designing churches as far afield as San Antonio, Texas and Dresden, Germany, always in the new well-established Neo-Gothic tradition. He is best known, however, as the architect for the Connecticut State Capitol in Hartford. Richard Mitchell's son, Hobard B. Upjohn, was the third member of this family to carry on a great tradition of superior architectural design.

The typical Gothic interior, complete with nave, side-aisle, apse, and clerestory illustrated the new Romanticism of the mid-nineteenth century.

First Baptist Church; Boston, Massachusetts

First Baptist Church
Commonwealth & Clarendon Streets
Boston, Masssachusetts 02116

Completed in 1871   **Henry H. Richardson, architect**

A handsome Lombard tower, though 176 feet high, stands somewhat modestly in the midst of a quiet residential area. It bears the unmistakable round-arch-rusticated-stone signature of Henry Hobson Richardson, father of the "Richardson-Romanesque" style, and the nation's first architect of international stature.

The tower of Boston's First Baptist Church is crowned with a frieze of over-life-size figures by Frederic Bartholdi, French sculptor of the Statue of Liberty. The figures were executed, *in situ,* by Italian artisans in 1871.

The interior is roofed over with an interesting system of rough-hewn wooden trusses, resembling the typical American barn. This feature is as much Early Christian as it is Romanesque, though it lacks the warm light that floods through the windows of its Mediterranean prototypes.

I instinctively looked for the warmth and comfort of the typical Romanesque church, but I was left with a feeling of restlessness, perhaps because the interior is quite dark.

Outside, I noticed a shallow buttress that articulates the corner of the tower facing the street. I was tempted to justify it, either structurally or stylistically, when I realized that it served no rational, logical nor structural purpose.

It was placed there simply and naturally, and with utter uselessness, with the same love that placed the circlet of trumpeting angels at the tower's top, and which gave the Bostonians the chance to name the edifice "The Church of the Holy Beanblowers."

There are innumerable contemporary churches that are sadly lacking in human touches of just this kind, and which remain, unfortunately, at an arm's length distance from their congregations.

Services: Sunday, 11 a.m.
Open to visitors: Monday to Friday, 9 a.m. to 12 noon, 1 to 4 p.m.
Seating Capacity: 650

An ecstatic burst of creativity and romanticism expressed itself in architecture, sculpture, and music.

Telephone: (617) 267-3148

Construction Cost: $200,000

How to get there: The church is located in the Back Bay area of Boston, at the corners of Commonwealth Avenue and Clarenden Street.

Architect: **Richardson, Henry Hobson.** 1833-1886. Born in Parish of St. James, Louisiana. Richardson was educated at Harvard University and the Ecole des Beaux Arts in Paris. Work represented: Trinity Episcopal Church (see page 39) and the First Baptist Church, both in Boston. Other important works: Albany City Hall, Libraries in Quincy, Massachusetts and Burlington, Vermont, Severn Hall and the Law School at Harvard, the Allegheny County Courthouse and the Marshall Field Warehouse in Chicago, and many residences in the "Shingle Style" of which he was a master. Richardson initiated the "Richardson-Romanesque" style. *The Architecture of America* by John Burchard and Albert Bush-Brown refers to Richardson as " . . . one of the few great American architects of all time."

First Lutheran Church
(Boston Lutheran Church)
299 Berkeley Street, Back Bay, Boston, Massachusetts 02116

Completed on September 15, 1957   **Pietro Belluschi, architect**

The First Lutheran Church does precisely what the church building was originally intended to do, but what many of the world's great churches do not do. It provides an ideal atmosphere for public and private worship and meditation without demanding – and distracting – the worshiper's attention by its architectural character.

Certainly this generation's foremost designer of religious buildings could have created a striking, challenging and exciting edifice. But rather than attempting a personal triumph, Belluschi created what Le Corbusier described and transcribed on the door of his famed chapel at Ronchamp, "a place of silence, of prayer, of spiritual joy."

Le Corbusier, needless to say, went far beyond his own program; he created an architectural shrine. Belluschi designed a simple, unassuming, totally unobtrusive structure without a crescendo of arches, vaults and buttresses, a design that disappears into its residential surroundings.

The interior is one of complete serenity: the warm rose brick of the exterior is repeated inside, blending with the natural wood and rough plaster ceiling. A single masterful touch goes almost unnoticed; at the top of the walls, a continuous band of clerestory lighting seems to lift the shallow vault of the concrete roof and render it weightless.

There are no statues, no colored glass, no murals. In one of Park Avenue's prestigious Jesuit churches I once found a pamphlet which stated, "Statues are permitted and encouraged because they arouse religious fervor." Neither Belluschi nor the building committee apparently felt that such decorative elements were essential to the success of their enterprise.

But the architect added one special feature. Immediately adjacent to the church and accessible to the outside there is an enclosed planted area, creating an atmosphere similar to that of the Romanesque cloister. Here, once again, the architect carefully avoided the demanding presence of any historic prototype. Anyone may enter here and meditate. On my recent visit, the garden was occupied by a young man, presumably during his lunch hour, whose meditations seemed to possess an unmistak-

First Lutheran Church; Boston, Massachusetts

ably transcendental quality.

Pietro Belluschi, who also designed the Priory Chapel in Portsmouth, Rhode Island (see page 131), was awarded the coveted Annual Gold Medal of the American Institute of Architects in 1970.

Services: Sunday, 8 and 11 a.m.
Open to visitors: Weekdays, 9:30 a.m. to 4:30 p.m.; July and August, 10 a.m. to 4 p.m.
Seating Capacity: 354
Telephone: (617) 536-8851
Construction Cost: $250,000
How to get there: The church is one block from Arlington Street (Public Gardens) and one block from Storrow Drive (Charles River).

Architect: **Belluschi, Pietro, FAIA.** Born in 1899 in Ancona, Italy. Former resident of Boston, now located in Portland, Oregon with his own firm. Works represented; Portsmouth Abbey Campus, Portsmouth, Rhode Island (see page 131) and Boston Lutheran Church. Other important works: Numerous churches, libraries, dormitories, schools, museums, banks and commercial buildings throughout New England. Belluschi has honorary degrees and awards from eleven American and foreign universities and museums. He was awarded Fellowship in 1968 and the Gold Medal in 1972 by the American Academy of Arts and Sciences, the National Academy of Design, and the Royal Academy of Fine Arts of Copenhagen, Denmark. He has received approximately forty-four architectural awards between 1938 and 1974.

Not a humble medieval shelter, an ornate Federal meetinghouse, nor a reflection of past architectural glories, the church reflects an atmosphere – anonymous, simple, and profound; one of prayer and devotion.

Trinity Episcopal Church; Boston, Massachusetts

The Boston bombshell

Trinity Episcopal Church
Copley Square, Boston, Massachusetts 02116

Completed on February 9, 1877   **Henry H. Richardson, architect**

The great cities of the western world are symbolized, almost without exception, by their major churches, because that is the image that first comes to mind when the name of a city is mentioned. In Paris, it is Notre Dame; London is identified by St. Paul's Cathedral, and Rome by St. Peter's Basilica. In Venice it is St. Mark's Cathedral; in Mexico City it is the Cathedral. Even Moscow, despite the gaping void between Church and State, is represented not so much by the forbidding walls of the Kremlin as by the colorful helical domes of St. Basil's Cathedral.

Boston is represented by Trinity Episcopal Church. Admittedly this ecclesiological gem, as an emblem, is matched by Bulfinch's historic State House and the splendidly renovated Quincy Market. But the persistence of the church, as an aspect of the city's manifold identity, is evidence of the power of religion in a world governed largely by politics and commerce. In my opinion, Trinity Church is the optimum example, in all of America, of this phenomenon. New York's Trinity Church is engulfed in the chasm of the city's financial district; St. Patrick's must compete with Rockefeller Center and the secular activities of the avenue that separates them. Washington's National Shrine, though it crowns the horizon like its English antecedents, stands aloof, and is not genuinely a living part of the activity of the Capitol.

Boston's Trinity Church, on the other hand, seems to share with its neighbors in the sense of history that is a visible and eloquent part of the city's charisma.

The evolution of Trinity Church is a fascinating chapter in the annals of American architecture. It began, like St. Peter's Basilica in Rome, with a competition. Six of the nation's foremost firms were invited " . . . to furnish a ground plan, three elevations, longitudinal and cross sections, a perspective drawing . . . and an approximate estimate not to exceed $200,000." All this was to be accomplished within the unbelievable space of six weeks! The memorable program further stated, "The Building Committee will pay you for your designs three hundred dollars. The plans become their property."

Only two of the resulting "six beautiful sets of plans" are in existence. They are clearly indicative of the high Victorian Gothic style prevailing at the time.

The premiated design by Louisiana-born and Harvard-trained Henry Hobson Richardson can be seen only through sketches, but it was undoubtedly identified by the audacious and highly personal version of Romanesque that characterized the final structure. Richardson was strongly influenced by his studies and travels in Western Europe. The major element, the central tower, can be traced to the Old Salamanca Cathedral in Spain; the West Porch, facing Copley Square, is clearly derived from the facade of St. Gilles-du-Gard in Provence. Though the West Porch plans were sketched by Stanford White, then an employee, and the latter designed by George Shepley after Richardson's death, the total concept is attributed to Richardson himself. The final design is an essentially personal version of the historic style on which it is based and is particularly noteworthy for its unity and consistency, despite the numerous changes made during its development.

Most importantly, Trinity Church sparked an esthetic explosion. A new "Style," in a century characterized by styles, was born, this one beginning with its own climax. Following the success of Trinity Church and other creations emanating from Richardson's prolific atelier, hundreds of churches, libraries, railroad stations, and public buildings appeared through the country bearing the stamp of "Richardson-Romanesque."

The widespread influence of the eponymous style that he created placed him in the ranks of Jose de Churriguera and Andrea Palladio. Henry Hobson Richardson, who died at the early age of 48, was America's first architect to receive international acclaim.

The scholarly official brochure, with an introduction by the rector, the Reverend Thom W. Blair, ends with, "The church, as they left it for future generations, is a masterpiece, a pleasant alliance of a brilliant architect, a talented designer, a sensitive and sympathetic Rector, and a knowledgeable, dedicated Building Committee. The church is a monument to the firm convictions of esthetic judgment and strong religious faith."

The purposely restrained summation is evidence that mere words and visual representations can in no way do justice to this extraordinary structure. To appreciate it, to evaluate it, to enjoy it, one must see it in its day-to-day context, with ample time to contemplate its significance. Only then can one realize how today's giant steel and glass towers seem to shrink in the background of its serene and timeless presence. Only then can one begin to sense the physical and spiritual stature of this splendid edifice.

Like Florence's Santa Croce and London's Westminster Abbey, Trinity Church, in the wealth of great names that are associated with it, is a pantheon of sorts. The rector at the time of its inception and for the following generation was the renowned Phillips Brooks, who later became bishop of Massachusetts. He laid the cornerstone on May 20, 1875:

**Old Salamanca Cathedral;
Salamanca, Spain**

**St. Gilles-du-Gard;
Provence, France**

he presided at the dedication of the completed building on February 9, 1877. His likeness is represented in three locations, including one by Augustus St. Gaudens and one by Daniel Chester French. Phillips Brooks is best known by name in the Boston area, but his 1867 composition, "O Little Town of Bethlehem," has reached many generations and may outlast Trinity Church itself.

The stained-glass windows in the Baptistry and in the north transept were designed by Sir Edward Burne-Jones and executed by William Morris, both prominent in London's Pre-Raphaelite movement. Richard Morris Hunt, one of the original competitors, and Charles McKim, of the nationally-known firm of McKim, Mead, and White, were members of the committee selected to review the designs made after Richardson's death. The latter firm was further distinguished by Stanford White, known for his non-architectural pursuits as well as for his achievements in the art of building.

The trapezoidal one-acre site was purchased in two sections for the total sum of $179,400. Richardson's estimate of the cost of construction was augmented by Norcross Brothers of Worcester, Massachusetts, by $6000 to $286,000. The expenditure for the total project finally amounted to $675,000.

John LaFarge was paid $8000 for his mural; Richardson's total fee, including his expenses, amounted to $7,218.19. Fortunately genius, vitality, and dedication cannot be measured in dollars. The true reimbursement to the creative soul can be evaluated only by the emotions aroused by the viewer, and their lasting impact on the city, on the profession, and on posterity. One might safely say that, in this respect, Richardson was well rewarded.

Services: Sunday, 8 and 11 a.m., 7 p.m.; Wednesday, 12:10 p.m.
Open to visitors: The church doors are open every day from 8 a.m. to 4 p.m.
Seating Capacity: 1350 to 1400
Telephone: (617) 539-0944
Construction Cost: $435,000 (see text)

How to get there: Trinity Church is situated at the east end of Copley Square, in Boston's Back Bay area. The Square is bounded by Boylston, Clarendon, and St. James Avenues, and Dartmouth Street. The nearest exit from the Turnpike is the Prudential Center exit.

Architect: **Richardson, Henry Hobson** (see page 34).

An esthetic explosion, dynamic, enveloping, exuberant, and resounding in its masses and proportions, it is a monument as much to the glory of the man He created as it is to God Himself.

Chapel at MIT; Cambridge, Massachusetts

The Chapel at
Massachusetts Institute of Technology (MIT)

Southeast corner of Massachusetts Avenue and Vassar Street
Cambridge, Massachusetts 02139

Completed in 1955   **Eero Saarinen, architect**

The university was born of the Church. It is not surprising, then, that a prominent feature of many great centers of learning is often an outstanding chapel.

King's College Chapel is the visual highlight of Cambridge University; the Church of the Sorbonne was Paris' first true dome. Even those centers dedicated to the military arts have provided special shelters for the rejuvenation of the spirit. West Point boasts a truly magnificent Gothic Revival chapel; a procession of spires in aluminum folded plates is the pride of the Air Force Academy in Colorado.

And Massachusetts Institute of Technology, in tacit acknowledgement of the mystical union between science and religion, has Saarinen's chapel.

According to Aline Saarinen's book on her husband's work, he wanted to create an atmosphere "where the individual could contemplate things larger than himself." The success of this ambitious program may be questioned on psychological grounds since the building, inside and out, bears the unmistakable personal stamp of its gifted creator, a quality which may detract from its universal appeal. And as a place "conducive to prayer," it cannot, in all fairness, claim precedence over thousands of other churches designed since the beginnings of Christian worship.

But it is without question another in Saarinen's long list of personal triumphs. Detail after detail bears witness to the genius of one of this century's greatest American architects.

The chapel is a simple cylinder, surmounted by a skeletal steel spire. This feature, by Theodore Reszak, instead of surmounting the structure at the center, is carefully located eccentrically. Were it not for this master stroke, the huge red brick drum might have resembled a giant firecracker.

One is invited inside through an aluminum-and-glass narthex, which Saarinen himself concedes is rather clumsy, to an interior that is a major architectural work.

The atmosphere inside literally glows. Natural light filters through

The key is light. The light illuminates shapes, and shapes have an emotional power.

the large oculus in the ceiling and is broken into tiny sparkling fragments as it bounces off the facets of Harry Bertoia's suspended bronze reredos, and light rises through the clerestory about the building's base as it is reflected upwards from the surface of the miniature moat that circles the chapel's exterior.

The interior walls, rather than repeating the geometric anonymity of the exterior, are gently undulated. There is a special feeling of comfort and intimacy, physical as well as spiritual, which belies the chapel's 130-pew capacity and its deceptive fifty-foot diameter.

Saarinen died suddenly at the age of fifty. One wonders what other churches would have enriched his *oeuvre*, had he lived, like both Frank Lloyd Wright and Christopher Wren, past the age of ninety!

Services: Multi-denominational services are held throughout the week.

Open to visitors: Daily, 7 a.m. to 11 p.m.

Seating Capacity: 130

Telephone: (617) 253-7973

Construction Cost: Not known.

How to get there: Take Massachusetts Avenue north over Harvard Bridge into Cambridge. MIT Chapel is just across the street on the left, in a grassy rectangle formed by Massachusetts Avenue, Memorial Drive, Vassar Avenue, and Danforth Street. Seize the first legal parking space and walk in.

Architect: **Saarinen, Eero,** FAIA. 1910-1961. Born in Finland. Son of internationally-known Eliel Saarinen. Saarinen was educated in Paris and at Yale University. Work represented: MIT Chapel. Other important works: Ingalls Hockey Rink and Stiles-Morse Colleges at Yale, TWA and Dulles International airports, General Motors Technical Center, Warren, Michigan, Memorial Arch, "Gateway to the West," St. Louis, Missouri, Research Center, Bell Laboratories, New Jersey CBS Building, New York. After Frank Lloyd Wright, Saarinen is considered America's most famous architect.

The Christian Science Center; Boston, Massachusetts

The enjoyment of urban design

Church of Christ, Scientist
The Christian Science Center
Massachusetts and Huntington Avenues, Back Bay
Boston, Massachusetts 02115

Completed in 1975

I.M. Pei & Partners
Cossuta and Ponte, architects
Aberthaw Construction Company, builder

Michelangelo gave urban design its name when he designed the famed Campidoglio in Rome in the sixteenth century. And in 1975 Io Ming Pei, Araldo Cossuta, and Vincent Pasciuto-Ponte brought it to a glorious climax in Boston's Christian Science Center.

Both Michelangelo and his contemporary colleagues also gave us the architectural definition of genius. The problem of integrating several seemingly unrelated existing buildings with additional contemporary structures on an odd-shaped site criss-crossed by traffic was the challenge that Michelangelo faced and is one that presents itself almost daily in today's growing and changing environment.

To conceal the lengthy litany of difficulties, frustrations and delays, and to blend every circumstance and unrelated factor into a living, inviting, esthetic whole can only be the result of genuine inspiration. And in this respect, Boston's Christian Science Center, like its Renaissance counterpart, is the *chef-d'oeuvre* of this century.

The center is not merely a "complex" of buildings, to use a somewhat contradictory modern term. Nor is it a square, a plaza, a place, a piazza or a platz. It is a center, and the only synonym to do it justice is the word "unit." It is a superb, functioning and esthetic whole, and it is this unity that the occasional passerby, the daily user, and the appraising historian enjoy to the fullest.

The Center is supremely satisfying. It gives one a sensation of pleasure; it provides a moment of repose, and it arouses a feeling of pride.

All these impressions are built into an architectural ensemble that is felt as soon as it is seen. And yet the Center is not made up of elements that are special in themselves. One cannot dissect it and examine it piece by piece with any satisfaction, any more than one might dissect the human body and evaluate its parts separately.

Nor can it be adequately summed up in words. The most comprehensive review, a veritable paean to this creation, was written by William Marlin for the September, 1977 issue of the now defunct *Architectural Forum*. The review is highly perceptive and, in terms of architectural criticism, definitive. Marlin, too, is mesmerized by the indescribable satisfaction that the Center arouses. And even so, he does not do it full justice.

Araldo Cossuta, the Center's designer, also acknowledges the problem. He terminates his personal and understandably inconclusive appraisal with the question, "What are the words we have tried to breathe into these inert building forms? We hope that they will convey a sense of community with the surroundings and a friendly message to all men. We hope that they will express the spirit of search and truth to which both religion and art are dedicated." It would be difficult to say better what, in the end, cannot adequately be put into words.

Parenthetically, Le Corbusier, world-renowned Swiss architect, attempted to do the same when he inscribed on the entrance door of his famed chapel at Ronchamp, "In this chapel, I wished to create a place of silence, of prayer, of peace, of spiritual joy." He went on to say, "A sense of the sacred animated our effort. Some things are sacred, others are not, whether they be religious or not."

The words relating to the outstanding religious structure of this century are those of an avowed atheist. It is understandable that a team composed of architects of Oriental and Roman Catholic backgrounds could design an equally inspired center for the Church of Christian Science.

The Matter of Style

The Center is made up of a great number of disparate elements. There are three existing buildings:

The Neo-Romanesque Mother Church, designed in 1894 by Franklin Welch; the Extension (the main place of worship), an Italian Baroque exterior and Byzantine interior, designed by Brigham and Beham in 1905; the Neo-Classic Christian Science Publishing Society Building in 1934.

Taking this melange of styles in their stride, I. M. Pei and his Associated Architects added, in 1975, the five-story curved Sunday School; the twenty-eight story Administration Building; the Church Colonnade Building, with five stories; the Neo-Roman portico addition to the extension; two separate landscape areas, one on Huntington Avenue, the other on Massachusetts Avenue. The former includes the reflecting pool, the circular fountain, and the 600-car underground parking garage.

The 1975 additions follow no particular "style" in the sense of a pre-established design formula. They belong to the immediate present, to be sure, but they do not impose a particular vocabulary on the neighborhood already resounding with a cacaphony of idioms.

On the other hand, the new buildings and their implacement possess great "style" in the sense of the term implying character, dignity, and the assurance of quality that does not rely on fixed symbols for its identity or its claim to permanence.

The new additions are parts of a beautifully coordinated whole, like the statues that distinguish the west portals of Chartres Cathedral. They are vertical and horizontal elements in a composition that is as satisfying, in the abstract sense, as the concrete from which they are formed.

The vertical Administration Building is an acknowledgement and a tie with the insistent verticals of the growing and dynamic city to the east. The long horizontal of the Colonnade Building and, of course, the pool itself, are a static suggestion of repose introduced to arrest the tendency toward undisciplined change that might otherwise take place under the guise of "progress."

It is the daring introduction of the reflecting pool, an area of alternating ripple and reflection, of motion and of rest, that brings the entire unit to life and which, along with the linden trees and the perennial planting, provide a breath of nature and eternity to a place which would otherwise be hastily traversed and forgotten.

The surface of the pool, longer than two football fields, flows gently, continuously and faultlessly over its rounded rim of polished Minnesota granite as the water aerates the Center's air conditioning system. It is a blend of art and science, of timeless esthetics and modern day engineering, of which Leonardo da Vinci would have approved most heartily.

A thirty-four acre project cannot help but invite comparisons. The least significant of these is the matter of project cost. The additions to the Center built by Pei and his associates are listed at the astonishingly low total of $55,000,000. In the light of the cost of labor and materials a mere half decade later, this sum seems totaly unreal.

The cost of this most recent paradigm of religious architecture compares with one of its historic prototypes, the first truly great Christian church. According to the historian Will Durant, the final tab for Santa Sophia in Constantinople, completed in 537 A.D., was 320,000 pounds (yes, pounds!) of gold. In terms of today's fluctuating exchange, this is somewhere in the neighborhood of a billion dollars, at the very least. Viewed in this light, the Christian Science Center may be one of history's greatest bargains.

Esthetic comparison with other examples of urban design are rewarding, and all are flattering.

Lincoln Center for the Performing Arts in New York City is another contemporary exercise in urban design, but despite the galaxy of great names associated with its conception, it is lacking in warmth and esthetic appeal and is generally considered of only minor architectural interest. Its function is broken into separate units, related only in their mutual proximity, and the Center comes to life only seasonally and intermittently.

Constitution Plaza in Hartford, well designed and magnificently sited, is removed from the mainstream of daily human activity, and the public as a whole cannot truly enjoy its unique setting and its impressive design features.

Albany's vast mall, which also enjoyed the opportunity to give beauty to our economic way of life, is a vast and forbidding wasteland that is admittedly an esthetic disaster.

One is impelled, unconsciously to return to history's famed centers

that focus on a religious structure.

St. Peter's Piazza is ponderous and distant, despite the fountains that brighten and enlighten it and the magnificent colonnade that embraces it.

The new *"parvis"* facing Notre Dame in Paris fares better. The cathedral is the central focus for a pleasant grassy area surrounded by historic buildings; it echoes the Center's acknowledgement of man's addiction to mobility with a vast underground park, this time at two levels.

A Startling Parallel

It is in Venice that one discovers the most flattering echoes of Boston's Center. The Renaissance arches of the Center's Extension, as they are mirrored in the surface of the pool, immediately recall the baroque palaces that line the Grand Canal. But it is in St. Mark's Square itself that one discovers the most surprising similarities between the two.

Although St. Mark's Square is bounded by works of art that span a near millenium, it is not their individuality but their unity, again, that makes the Square a unique experience. One need not check off the styles, from the cathedral's Byzantine domes and Sansovino's Library, to the 1910 replica of the original Campanile, to relish the full esthetic experience and to appreciate the remarkable similarity to the Boston Center.

Nor is it necessary to savor the miracles in mosaic that line the piers and pendentives of the interior, or the vast halls and the theatrical

52

ambience of the cortile of the Ducal Palace to appreciate the full ecstacy of St. Mark's Square itself.

One enjoys the individual parts without even being aware of the vertical of the Campanile as opposed to the horizontal of the arcaded business structures or, for that matter, the almost arbitrary placing of the two classic columns across the horizontal of the Adriatic itself. It is gratifying, incidentally, to learn that the Adriatic has graciously and permanently receded.

It is the supreme satisfaction of the entire composition, rather than the intrinsic artistic validity of its parts, in both St. Mark's Square and Boston's Christian Science Center, that elevates urban design to the level of great art. One can imagine how the grandeur of St. Paul's Cathedral in London would have been enhanced by the setting that it was denied when Wren's city plan was rejected.

The purpose of the art of urban design, to paraphrase a dictum attributed to the painter, Picasso, is enjoyment. And to the vast daily crowds that visit St. Mark's Square, and Boston's Christian Science Center (and, for that matter, Florida's Disneyworld), it is just that simple.

Services: Sunday, 10:45 a.m., 7:30 p.m.; Sunday School, 10:45 a.m.; Wednesday, 7:30 p.m.
Open to visitors: Monday to Saturday, 10 a.m. to 3:30 p.m.; Sunday, 12 to 3:30 p.m.
Seating Capacity: 4000
Telephone: (617) 262-2300
Construction Cost: $82.7 million (see text)
How to get there: Follow Huntington Avenue south from the Prudential Center exit off the Massachusetts Turnpike. The Christian Science Center is on the right shortly beyond the Prudential Center complex.

Architect: **Pei, Ieoh Ming,** FAIA, RIBA. Born in Canton, China in 1917. Pei earned degrees from Massachusetts Institute of Technology and the Harvard Graduate School of Design. Work represented: Christian Science Center, Boston, Massachusetts. Other important works: Museums and arts centers in Washington D.C., Boston, Massachusetts, Cambridge, Massachusetts, Ithaca, New York, Syracuse, New York, Wallingford, Connecticut, Des Moines, Iowa. Educational buildings: Rochester, New York, Cambridge, Massachusetts, Columbia, New York, Syracuse, New York. Libraries in Columbus, Indiana, Boston, Massachusetts, Government Buildings in Oklahoma City, Oklahoma, Bank Buildings in Singapore and Denver, Colorado. Also numerous other buildings and urban centers. He has also received honorary degrees from seven American universities; fellowship in the American Institute of Architects in 1972; the Gold Medal of the American Institute of Academy of Arts and Letters, and the Gold Medal of the American Institute of Architects in 1979, as well as many other national awards, Gold medals, fellowships and citations.

West Parish Meetinghouse; West Barnstable, Massachusetts

West Parish Meetinghouse

(United Church of Christ)
Meetinghouse Way, Rte. 419
W. Barnstable, Massachusetts 02668

Completed in 1719 (Restored in 1956)   **Architect Unknown**

"The oldest Congregational building in America."

"One of the two surviving First Period Meetinghouses" (the other is Hingham's Old Ship Meetinghouse, see page 3).

These somewhat impersonal references have the quality of *déjà vu;* very few churches in New England are without their list of "firsts" and "onlys."

But Barnstable's "Rooster-Church" has numerous other distinguishing qualifications. "It is not a museum, but a monument . . ." to Elizabeth Crocker Jenkins, a member of that dynasty of rare souls who offer themselves, generously and selflessly, to the preservation of our past glories. Due largely to her efforts, West Parish Congregational Church ranks, though at a smaller scale, along with Williamsburg and Jamestown as one of the nation's masterpieces of architectural restoration.

The result is specially noteworthy in that it does not attempt to reflect its age and weathering. The clean look and the smell of the newly-hewn beams and the recently-turned spindles, colored by the sunlight that falls through the new double-hung windows, must closely approximate the atmosphere that welcomed the worshipers on the day of dedication on Thanksgiving, 1719.

The interior is warm, intimate and a beautifully proportioned unit. I am not entirely at home with the social implications of the "sheep-pen" pews which appear in the gallery as well as on the main floor. I wonder if this is precisely what Henry Jacob had in mind when he and his friends joined hands in 1616 in the borough of Southwark and founded the Congregational Church, adding another variation to Christian worship and imprinting it upon the architectural character of New England?

Another unanswered question concerns the jaunty gilded cock that adorns the top of the tower. Who commissioned it? Who fabricated it? And who established its five-foot by five-inch dimensions, that seem perfectly proportioned to the ensemble, as it gleams in the morning sun?

And why a cock? Why not an eagle or an owl? Does the sly note of

The church is a labor of love, resulting in a spectacular renovation.

Protestant symbolism refer to Peter's denial of Christ? Edmund Sinnott refers to the cock as the "Puritan symbol of repentance," but it is difficult to reconcile its defiant stance with any suggestion of contrition. The cock surely has nothing whatever to do with its Gallic cousin who crows daily from every town hall in France. This feature remains one of symbolism's minor puzzles.

But it is a detail that adds to a thoroughly rewarding detour for anyone going anywhere on Cape Cod. It is open to visitors from nine to five. And free.

Services: Sunday, 9:50 a.m.
Seating Capacity: 350
Open to visitors: Decoration to Labor Day, 9 a.m. to 5 p.m.
Telephone: (617) 362-4445
Construction Cost: Unknown.
How to get there: Follow Route 6A north from Barnstable to first traffic light. Then turn left. The church is one-quarter of a mile down Route 149.

Architect: **Unknown.**

West Parish Meetinghouse

First Church of Christ, Unitarian; Lancaster, Massachusetts

First Church of Christ (Unitarian)
Town Common, Lancaster, Massachusetts 01523

Completed on January 1, 1817   **Charles Bulfinch, architect**

The name "Lancaster" evokes numerous images. It recalls a colorful chapter in England's medieval past. It represents the locale of the devout, hardworking and prosperous religious communities of western Pennsylvania. It is less widely known as the identification of one of the high points in the history of the nation's churches.

The First Unitarian Church in Lancaster, Massachusetts, was designed by the renowned Charles Bulfinch, one of the last of the gentleman-amateur architects and America's first professional practitioner.

Boston-born and Harvard-educated, Bulfinch designed government buildings, libraries, theatres, and residences throughout the Boston area. He also designed at least five churches, only two of which are still in existence. The other one is St. Stephen's Church in Boston (see page 11).

The town of Lancaster itself is a visitor's dream. Had the Massachusetts Turnpike chosen to tread its inexorable way twenty miles to the north of Worcester, the town of Lancaster as we see it, would certainly not have survived. But thanks to geography and the sheer objectivity of civil engineering, this handsome town has been left relatively intact. Lancaster is approached, not by a busy highway, but by an avenue shaded by oaks and maples, lined with stately homes beyond broad, well-kept lawns.

The approach to the town is climaxed by the ample, well proportioned green which is a revelation. In its layout and in the orientation and the quality of the buildings that face it on three sides, it resembles a self-conscious stage set; in actuality, however, it is the cultural and religious center of a quiet but thriving community.

The green is crowned, but not overwhelmed, by the church itself. One is struck immediately by the fact that the church seems to fall in place gracefully, without effort. It is no surprise to learn that its exact location was the subject of heated debate among town officials until its final location was "determined," through arbitration, by a third party.

The church is only a single element in what is a superb exercise in urban design. It cannot be separated from the library, the town offices, and its relation to the access avenue. All the elements of the town's composition are part of an eminently satisfying whole and are eloquent testimony to the fact that the now famous church was not the result of a specific religious need but a civic project in which the entire community participated.

In this respect, Lancaster's church is the archetype of the New England meetinghouse, which performed various community functions until well into the nineteenth century.

Architecturally, however, it is the least "typical" of its entire age. It is made up, to be sure, of all the standard components, including the entrance portico, the belfry, the auditorium with the gallery on three sides. But from the point of view of design, in comparison to its Connecticut and Rhode Island neighbors, it is a resounding breakthrough.

Providence's First Baptist Meetinghouse (see page 125), already more than a generation old, was assembled from well-documented English prototypes; Connecticut's graceful solutions were likewise derived from Neo-Classic and Palladian examples imported, courtesy of Wren and Gibbs, by Hoadley, Town, and Benjamin.

Lancaster's Unitarian Church, on the other hand, owes nothing to a pre-arranged text or tradition. It was designed throughout by a gifted architect who conformed solely to the logical dictates of firmness, commodity, and delight as expounded by Rome's Marcus Vitruvius Pollio, and then proceeded to instill it with his own genius.

Structurally, the church follows the tradition of soundness as expressed by the master builders of the times. Functionally, it responds to the combined requirements of the community and the congregation.

Esthetically, it reflects the ability of a creative mind who saw the problem as one of balance, scale, proportion, discrimination, form, texture, color, detail, and taste, and combined them into a single wholly satisfying esthetic unit.

In its ensemble, the church is nothing short of perfection. One has only to read the pages devoted to it in William Pierson's *American Buildings and Their Architects*, in which he ascends to heights of appreciation that border on poetry. It was Pierson, incidentally, who designated Bulfinch's Lancaster Church as "an American Masterpiece."

Lancaster's First Church contains, in addition, that special element that arouses public appreciation and endears it to the architectural critic. This is the element of surprise, a subtle form of flattery that elevates both the creator and his audience in their mutual esteem and leaves both with a special brand of esthetic satisfaction.

Bulfinch, first of all, abandoned the Wren's Gothic-inspired spire in favor of the dome. Then he abandoned the ornate Roman portico and introduced the brick arches, outlined by Doric pilasters. He then skillfully tied the whole composition together with a continuous cornice.

In his consistent refinement and restraint, he presaged the Greek Revival. The interior is not architecturally significant. It is, indeed,

The interior is rarely matched in unity and serenity, and is, to my knowledge, unsurpassed.

rather plain, except for the relatively ornate pulpit with its Ionic and Corinthian details that seem to contradict the message of the purposely restrained exterior.

But a single element distinguishes the auditorium in a way that no other meetinghouse can match. Since its dedication in 1816, Lancaster's Unitarian Church has been heated by two cast-iron wood-burning stoves. The black stovepipes, ten inches in diameter, do not rise directly to the ceiling; they rise to a height of nine feet, then run horizontally with a slight pitch, suspended the length of the auditorium to a point just short of the pulpit, where they rise and disappear into the white plaster ceiling.

The exposed stovepipes are a startling feature to say the least. And yet, this is an example, clothed in the most primitive form, of radiant heating, the most sophisticated method of distribution. In the most rational sense, it is yesterday's clear response to today's need for efficiency and the conservation of natural resources. To compare the cost of heating the Lancaster Church quickly and efficiently for brief, occasional uses, with more "modern" methods would be ludicrous. Furthermore, the use of exposed pipes and ducts as design features, a current trend in schools, banks, shopping malls, (not to mention the Centre Pompidou in Paris) brings Bulfinch's church surprisingly up-to-date.

The presence of a Bulfinch project so far removed from the large active centers of population is the result of an interesting coincidence. Bulfinch, though a Protestant, designed Boston's first Roman Catholic church when Father James Thayer was its priest (one is reminded that Le Corbusier, though an avowed atheist, was selected to design the now famous Roman Catholic shrine at Ronchamp). Father James Thayer's grand-nephew, Nathaniel Thayer, was pastor of the Lancaster congregation; the recommendation of Bulfinch as architect was, in a sense, preordained.

Curiously, though Charles Bulfinch is credited with the design and detail of the Lancaster church, there is no evidence that he ever visited the site during the construction period. Thomas Hersey, well-known master-builder of Boston, moved to nearby Harvard to act as construction superintendent. Presumably, if he made any decisions on his own, they must have been the correct ones.

Lancaster's Unitarian church, listed as the "First Church of Christ" in its National Landmark designation, is most often referred to, without irreverence, as "The Bulfinch Church."

Services: Sunday, 11 a.m.
Seating Capacity: 1000.
Open to visitors: Sundays, or by appointment.
Telephone: (617) 365-2427
Construction Cost: $20,000

How to get there: From Boston, follow Route 2 or Route 117 to Lancaster. Turn south on Main Street. From west or south, follow Route I-95 north to Route 117, then south on Main Street for one mile.

Architect: **Bulfinch, Charles** (see page 12).

Methodist Tabernacle; Oak Bluffs, Massachusetts

"Surely the Lord is in this place!"

Methodist Tabernacle
Oak Bluffs, Massachusetts 02557

Completed in 1879   **John Hoyt, George Dwight, architects**
John Hoyt, builder

In Classic times, the inhabitants of Hellas made fortnight-long visits
to Delphi to savour the beauties of the temple, the stimulation of the
theatre, and the excitement of the stadium, not to mention a visit to
the Oracle. Meanwhile they enjoyed the intoxicating atmosphere and
the sweep of the natural setting.

In the Middle Ages, people went on pilgrimages, long after the disastrous crusades, to assure themselves of special consideration in the
hereafter, and also to seek relief from the tedium of life on the farm and
in the village.

Today millions of Moslems look forward to at least one visit to the
Holy City of Mecca, again for a multitude of reasons.

In the nineteenth century, following similar impulses, the
Methodists went to their renowned "Camp meetings." Of these, the best-
known, the most colorful, and the most historically significant took
place in the village of Oak Bluffs on Martha's Vineyard. And their outward symbol is the famed "Tabernacle."

Here is a structure where not only architecture, engineering, and the
environment meet in glorious unison, but religion, service to mankind,
and human psychology are likewise fully represented.

The Tabernacle is an open pavilion, rising with two levels of
clerestory windows to a cupola which serves as a design feature as well
as a huge exhaust for the accumulation of warm air. In mass and in
detail it is as imaginative as John Nash's Brighton Pavilion (1820), as
structurally important as the Eiffel Tower (1887) and the Brooklyn
Bridge (1883). It is an exaggerated folie with a serious purpose; it is a
gazebo to end all gazebos. And it is also a national treasure.

The tabernacle was primarily a place of worship. When the first
Camp meeting was held there on August 24, 1835, only several hundred
persons were present. They worshiped in a large central tent and spent
the night in small tents around the periphery of Wesleyan Grove.

The meetings grew in population and in popularity. In 1869, according to the brochure, "more than 30,000 persons visited the camp
grounds, attracted by the walk, the berrying, the fishing, the boating,

Artistry can be seen in the wrought iron, first developed by and for the marketplace, now in the service of religion.

and the swinging . . ." In 1879 the present structure was built by the firm of Hoyt and Wright of Springfield, Mass., for a total cost of $7,147.84. The metal structure was selected after bids for a wood structure, ranging from $10,000 to $15,000, were rejected.

Its capacity is approximately 2000. It measures 100 feet to the top of the cupola and is 130 feet in diameter. Today it is used throughout the season of good weather for inspirational gatherings, graduation ceremonies, and rock concerts. It is an attraction for the architectural historian as well as for the tourist. It is set in a circlet of one-story wooden cottages which are the apotheosis of the Gingerbread Period. The ensemble rivals. Disneyworld in charm and surpasses it in authenticity.

The word "tabernacle" is first mentioned in the twenty-fifth chapter of *Exodus* in the Old Testament. According to the detailed description, it was a glorified tent. The Oak Grove tabernacle is also a glorified tent. The strict Methodist adherence to the text of the Bible explains their adoption of the term "tabernacle" despite the fact that, etymologically, it is directly derived from the Greek word for "wineshop."

But why the Methodists chose to erect a simple shelter with open sides is not entirely clear. They might have chosen to build a pretentious shrine, like the one at Knock in Ireland. Or even a Basilica, like the one at Guadalajara in Mexico or at Lourdes in France.

If we can extrapolate from today's records, they could have afforded it. *The World's Great Religions*, published by Life in 1957, lists assets of $2.7 billion for some 11.8 million U.S. Methodists, while the 33.4 million

U.S. Catholics rate second with a paltry $2 billion.

It is evident that they selected a relatively "functional" structure for their own sound reasons. Happily, the design did not fall into the miasma of derivative styles prevalent throughout the U.S. at the time. (Louis Sullivan's diatribes against the Beaux Arts influence had not achieved their impact, and Frank Lloyd Wright, in 1879, was only twelve years old.)

The simplest explanation, to me, seems eminently adequate. The Methodists did not need a monument. Even today, they are, of all denominations, among those who rely least on outward fixtures and accoutrements for their inspiration.

Perhaps they are unconsciously acknowledging the message of John Wesley himself, who for many years preached in the open fields. Accompanied by the brisk fresh air that sweeps off the sea, the experience of Oak Bluffs is refreshing in a multitude of ways. Indeed, Wesley may at this moment be looking benevolently upon the panorama where, instead of frozen images and static scenes in stained-glass, the flicker of thousands of Japanese lanterns in the evening light up the entire area, like the tongues of flame that once bore the message of the Holy Spirit.

Services: Sunday, 9:30 a.m., July and August.
Seating Capacity: 1800 to 2000
Open to visitors: The grounds are open at all times.
Telephone: None.
Construction Cost: $7,147.84
How to get there: The Tabernacle is situated in Wesleyan Grove, practically in the center of the town of Oak Bluffs.

Architects: **John Hoyt's** and **George Dwight's** biographies not available.

Holy Cross Church; Holyoke, Massachusetts

Old English Gothic in New England

Holy Cross Church

23 Sycamore Street, Holyoke, Massachusetts 01040

Completed on April 29, 1928 **John W. Donohue, architect**
Daniel O'Connell's Sons, builder

Holy Cross Church is the focal point of a spectacular view which, from Route 91, encompasses the entire valley, with the town and church as its dominating image.

Holyoke's major Gothic edifice, in certain respects, is the identical twin of St. Mary's Church in Stamford, and is St. Mary's diametric opposite in others. The two churches rival each other in authenticity, in prominence, and in the feeling of awe that their Gothic silhouettes inspire.

But while St. Mary's Church rises serene, but somewhat apprehensive, in an ambience of total economic deterioration, Holy Cross Church rests, majestic and self-assured in a well-kept and prosperous residential entourage. The handsome massive structure has been comfortably set into a spacious, well-kept lawn accented with maples and elms, in full justice to its unmistakable English ancestry.

The interior was altered in 1970 to conform to the renewed Roman Catholic liturgy by the Rambusch Company of New York, a firm internationally known for their combined engineering skill and artistic ability, particularly in interior lighting. The focus of the design is the church's eponymous symbol represented, not in oak (in acknowledgement of its vicinity) but in reflecting crystal prisms set in the center of a huge stainless steel nimbus.

The effect is powerful, but in the scale of the church, it is not in the least obtrusive. The design does not boast the esthetic challenges of the striking bronze reredos in St. Mark's Church in New Canaan, nor does it suffer, on the other hand, from the latter's somewhat distracting effect.

The use of metal to represent rays of light recalls Bernini's frequent use of this decorative feature, notably in St. Peter's Seat in the Basilica in Rome. A comparison of the one in Rome with the one in New Canaan is an eloquent definition of the difference between American Neo-Gothic and Italian Baroque.

The music of the organ in Holy Cross Church, as it fills and refills the variety of interconnecting spaces which are the essence of Gothic architecture, adds an additional dimension to this built-in drama of liturgical architecture and art which has few contemporary parallels.

Services: Sunday, 7, 8, 9, 10:15, and 11:30 a.m., 5:15 p.m.; Daily masses, 6:45 a.m. and 5:15 p.m.

Seating Capacity: 1100 to 1200

Open to visitors: Daily, 6:30 a.m. to 6 p.m.

Telephone: (413) 532-5661

Construction Cost: $450,000

How to get there: Take Exit 17A from Route I-91. Proceed to Pleasant Street on Dwight Street. Cross Pleasant Street and take the first right onto Holy Cross Avenue.

Architect: **Donohue, John.** Deceased. Biography not available.

A blend of the old and the new liturgy, the interior resounds in a concert of stone, steel, and crystal.

Church of the Blessed Sacrament; Holyoke, Massachusetts

The church around the world

Church of the Blessed Sacrament

1945 Northampton Street, Holyoke, Massachusetts 01040

Completed on April 5, 1943 **Charles F. Wright, architect**
Daniel O'Connell's Sons, builder

Holyoke's "Round Church" was one of the first in New England to break
with the age-old tradition of rectangular floor plans. This novel creation,
according to the church brochure, was "born of episcopal courage"
when Bishop Christopher Waldon of Springfield urged the building of a
"modern" church. Designed by Charles F. Wright, architect of Waltham,
Massachusetts, Blessed Sacrament Church was completed in 1953, and
was immediately internationally publicized. It served as a stepping-stone
to a rich variety of church plans long before the liturgical liberation that
was sparked by Vatican II.

The well-proportioned exterior in buff brick is surmounted by a
disc-like concrete roof and crowned by a skylight which, along with the
exterior fenestration, fills the interior with light and gives a sense of

weightlessness to the entire building. The peripheral seating focuses the attention on the ingenious crucifix that has not one, but two separate faces, back to back, thus obviating the psychological objection to participation in the Mass "from the back."

Blessed Sacrament Church has been publicized in eighty-eight countries and has received inquiries from Australia, Liberia, Korea, Ireland, Honolulu, and Panama, as well as over 100 American cities. This may be why it is sometimes referred to, in a nice play on words, as "The Church Around the World."

Despite one's first impression, Blessed Sacrament Church is not "round." It is octagonal in plan, and responds to an impressive list of historic prototypes. Charlemagne's three-story chapel at Aix-la-Chapelle, built in 792 through 805, is octagonal in plan. It was presumably inspired by Ravenna's San Vitale, erected in 330 A.D., which was, in turn, influenced by Rome's decagonal Minerva Medica, dated 260 A.D. (The latter was designed as a "Nymphaeum," a sanctuary dedicated to the lesser pagan goddesses.).

Furthermore, though the product of an age of advanced technology, it lacks the geometric sophistication of Rome's Santa Costanza, built in 468 A.D. and San Stefano Rotondo (468 A.D.), which are not only circular in plan, but topped by impressive masonry domes. And any of the above could fit comfortably within the spherical interior of Rome's Pantheon, whose height and diameter both are a staggering 142'-6". Fortunately, the architect did not rely on outward pretensions or space-age images to respond fully to Bishop Waldon's request. Holyoke's Round Church has grown from 150 families in 1953 to its present impressive roster of well over 6000 souls.

The unconscious tendency to associate its distinctive form with space exploration is not in the least pejorative. The ultimate aim of the church, from the start, is to release man from his terrestrial bondage. And in that respect a disc may well be infinitely more suitable than a Roman dome or a Gothic spire.

Services: Sunday, 8, 9:15, 10:30, and 11:45 a.m.; Daily, 6:45 a.m. and 5:20 p.m.; Saturday, 8 a.m., 4, 5:30, and 7:30 p.m.

Seating Capacity: 750

Open to visitors: Daily, 6:30 a.m. to 8:30 p.m.

Telephone: (413) 532-0713

Construction Cost: $350,000

How to get there: From Exit 16 on Route I-91, go two blocks east on Cherry Street to Northampton Street. Then go one-half mile south on Northampton.

Architect: **Wright, Charles F.** Deceased. Biography not available.

Chapel of Saint James the Fisherman; Wellfleet, Massachusetts

"I will make you fishers of men."

Chapel of Saint James the Fisherman
Route 6, south of Wellfleet Center
Wellfleet, Massachusetts 02667

Completed in 1957   **Olav Hammarstrom, architect**

The image of the Apostle James, brother of John, appears most often as a warrior and patron saint of Spain. He is also frequently represented, especially in art, as a pilgrim identified by a cockleshell (the original Coquille St. Jacques), leading the penitents from the Tour St. Jacques in Paris to the great Romanesque shrine at Santiago, in Spain's north-western extremity. Both roles are supported largely by legend. But James' occupation as a fisherman has never been questioned. And it is this aspect of his multiple personality that has been immortalized in architecture at the tip of Cape Cod.

In 1954 a small group of summer residents met with Dean James Pike (later diocesan Bishop of the Diocese of California), who became the guiding spirit in the building of the chapel. They proposed to erect a simple shelter for their summer devotions, a project to be characterized by a minimum of pretensions and a maximum of anonymity.

Mr. and Mrs. Carey E. Melville gave two acres of land to the project. The extent of this gift can easily be assessed in any Cape Cod real estate office. Olav Hammarstrom, Finnish-born and internationally experienced, donated his services as architect, interior designer, and sculptor, at no fee, while his wife Marianne Strengell of the Cranbrook School in Michigan offered her services as designer of textiles and color consultant. Paul Weidlinger, well-known New York engineer, served as structural consultant, also without charge.

The result of this felicitous association is a monument to restraint and taste. Wellfleet's chapel is not a publicly acclaimed masterpiece. It is not heralded by distant spires, nor is it graced by a vast paved esplanade. Indeed, those innumerable latter-day pilgrims who travel almost within its shadow to worship the pagan sun at Provincetown may not be aware of the chapel's existence. It is this quality that lends the Fisherman Chapel its greatest appeal.

The low rectangle of the body of the chapel is sheltered from the passing world by a screen of evergreens whose conical profiles are echoed by the shingled wooden spire. It is a quiet unobtrusive retreat from the hyperactive summer life which characterizes this part of the world.

The design as a whole avoids identification with any particular architectural "style." And yet it is a graphic, though certainly unintentional, definition of a phrase made famous by Mies van der Rohe. It was he who summed up an entire architectural philosophy in the cogent words "Less is more." James, son of Zebedee, must be especially pleased.

———

Services: Last Sunday in June to second Sunday in September, 9:30 a.m.; July and August, 7:30 a.m.
Seating Capacity: 320
Open to visitors: By appointment only.
Telephone: (617) 349-2690
Construction Cost: Unknown.
How to get there: The Chapel is located off Route 6, one and one-quarter miles south of Wellfleet Center.

Architect: **Hammarstrom, Olav.** Born in Heinola, Finland in 1906. Education: Diploma in Architecture, University of Technology, Helsinki, Finland; diploma from Athens, Greece. He was formerly associated with the offices of Alvar Aalto, Saarinen & Associates, Roche & Dinkeloo, and the Architects Collaborative. Work represented: Chapel of St. James the Fisherman, Wellfleet, Massachusetts, which received the American Institute of Architecture Design Award for 1958. Other Important Works: Churches in Amherst, Massachusetts, Hazel Park, Michigan, Oakridge, New Jersey, Nashua, New Hampshire, Lafayette, Georgia, and numerous residences in Connecticut, Massachusetts, Michigan, Ohio, Alabama, Georgia, and Canada.

A simple wood meetinghouse, the chapel's interior forms a square oculus to frame the light.

Pierce Chapel, Cranwell Academy; Lenox, Massachusetts

A temple without a cornerstone

Pierce Chapel, Cranwell Academy
55 Lee Road, Lenox, Massachusetts 01240

Completed in 1966   **Peter McLaughlin, architect**

The visitor to Lenox's famed music festivals may not realize that an architectural microcosm, symbolizing the full range and complexity of the human experience, lies hidden behind the majestic oaks and maples of nearby Cranwell Academy. It is the Michael Pierce Chapel, inspired by the Jesuit Father Mackin in 1965, a product of genius, imagination, and above all, faith. This unique structure embodies a host of revealing and contradictory symbols. The chapel is dedicated to Christ, not the King nor the Teacher, but the Servant.

Its plan is neither rectangular nor circular, but elliptical. Construction is not in traditional wood, brick, or stone, but in reinforced concrete. The focal point of the interior, crowned, like pagan Rome's Pantheon, by an oculus, is a crucifix designed by the well-known sculptor, Leonard Baskin, whose father was a rabbi. And after less than a decade of use, this renowned edifice is now being offered for sale for secular purposes.

Cranwell Academy was founded in 1939 by the Jesuit Order for the education of boys of preparatory school age. For four decades services were held in one of the community rooms. In 1968, as if by magic, a donor, an inspired, dedicated architect, a patient and obliging builder, and several gifted artists, together produced a powerful symbol of a simple belief in worship and community service.

The Michael Pierce Chapel, situated against the challenging background of the Berkshires, is a vibrant, pulsating creation. Its architect was Irish-born Peter McLaughlin, who had been associated with Bauhaus-trained Marcel Breuer in the design of the famed Benedictine Chapel in Collegeville, Minnesota.

McLaughlin created a twenty-eight-faceted jewel in reinforced concrete which, set against the incomparable background of the Berkshires, is alone worthy of an architectural pilgrimage. The rough concrete exterior is in striking contrast to the warm brick and terra cotta of the main school structure. The interior is a revelation. Giant reinforced concrete cantilevers, their haunches set firmly into the elliptical foundation, thrust their incredibly light arms toward the sanctuary. But instead of

The design is of a sophisticated elliptical skeleton, with a round oculus.

seeking mutual support, they terminate, miraculously balanced between earth and space, at the edge of a large central skylight through which light literally pours over the altar. The ultimate effect, reinforced by the sloping floor and the circular seating, is one of total physical, psychological and spiritual unity.

The outstanding feature of the interior, however, is the sequence of translucent trapezoidal panels that fill the spaces between the structural frames. They are not decorated with traditional "stained" glass in place with lead cames. Nor are they made of the currently fashionable "faceted" or "chipped" or "chunk" glass which is held together, separate and immobile, in rigid concrete. They consist of an ingenious system of individual irregularly-shaped panes, captured in a light steel network so that they overlap but do not touch. The result is a three-dimensional montage that sparkles with every change of outside light and the shifting position of the viewer as well. And fire from heaven, in all its chromatic manifestations from cold blue to searing yellow to gleaming orange to raging red, capturing but not replacing the rhythm of the season, filters through to comfort, to reassure, to inspire and to challenge man, just as it has for an eternity of centuries. These remarkable creations, a new abstract phase in the ever-expanding palette of esthetic expression, are the work of the designer Joseph Ferguson.

In its total context, like many throughout history that have preceded it, the Cranwell Chapel is evidence of the fact that its true substance is not its immediate and temporal presence, but the infinite spirit that was its inspiration. It is worship in all its manifestations, not the architecture itself, that gives religious architecture its ultimate meaning. The true significance of a great work lies not in its realization or its longevity, but in the spirit that brought it into existence.

Services: Sunday, 10:30 a.m.
Seating Capacity: 700
Open to visitors: Daily, 8 a.m. to 3 p.m.
Telephone: (413) 637-1030 (residence); (413) 637-0724 (groundskeeper)
Construction Cost: $1 million
How to get there: The chapel is two miles from the Lee exit off the Massachusetts Turnpike, and is forty-five minutes west of Springfield, Massachusetts.

Architect: **McLaughlin, Peter F.** Born in Ireland in 1927. Education: Attended the National University of Ireland, and is a member of the Royal Institute of British Architects. He now resides in Concord, New Hampshire, and is president of the Boston-based firm of Peter McLaughlin Associates.

First Congregational Church; Old Bennington, Vermont

First Congregational Church

Monument Avenue, Old Bennington, Vermont 05201

Completed in January 1806   **Lavius Fillmore, architect**

Lavius Fillmore, a native of Norwich, Connecticut, and a second cousin of Millard Fillmore, was not a trained architect, nor is he listed among the "gentlemen-amateurs" of the Federal Period. He was a builder. But he was responsible for the design and construction of two, and possibly three, of Vermont's outstanding meetinghouses.

Best known is the Congregational Church in Old Bennington, erected in 1805, closely following Plate 33 of Asher Benjamin's *Country Builder's Assistant.* This well-proportioned and beautifully-sited structure is appropriately described in William Pierson's *American Buildings and Their Architects* in his characteristically subjective style.

> It displays all the proportional and environmental features of the Federal style. It rises in provincial elegance before a shaded common to form a focal point in one of those ravishing fragments of early nineteenth century New England which have somehow escaped the intrusion of the late nineteenth century industrial erosion.

The interior transcends the limitations of the Federal style in variety and elegance. It is an exquisite free-flowing sculptural unit, perhaps the most beautiful meetinghouse of all of New England.

The church originally contained a separate section of pews with sides seven feet high, which were reserved for Negroes. In another section, the unmarried men have diligently carved their initials on the sides of the pews for posterity's record.

Services: Sunday, 11 a.m.
Seating Capacity: 650
Open to visitors: With guide, July 1 to mid-October, 10 a.m. to 4 p.m.
Telephone: (802) 447-1223
Construction Cost: $7793
How to get there: Drive west from Bennington on Route 9 for one-half mile. The church is 200 yards on the left.

Architect: **Fillmore, Lavius.** Born in 1757 in Norwich, Connecticut. Works represented: First Congregational Church in Bennington, Vermont and the Congregational Church in Middlebury, Vermont (see page 85). Little is known of his training and his private life.

Congregational Church; Middlebury, Vermont

Congregational Church

(Union Church of Christ)

Main Street, Middlebury, Vermont 05753

Completed in 1809   **Lavius Fillmore, architect**

Fillmore's second outstanding church is Middlebury Congregational. The portico is almost identical to Bennington's, and the tower is similar, though somewhat heavier. The Middlebury church is situated rather precariously on a sloping site, and its intrinsic tranquility is marred by the busy street that separates it from the green. Its white clapboard profile coexists, not inharmoniously, with its Episcopal neighbor in grey brick, the nearby United Methodist in red sandstone, the Baptist in grey granite, and the Knights of Columbus in red brick with white limestone trim. The variety of religious experiences, all within a stone's throw of each other, is a colorful witness to the Bill of Rights.

Middlebury's church was used as a chapel by Middlebury College until the late 1800s, and the last commencement was held there in 1935. It is still the locale of the annual December 12th celebration of Forefathers' Day, when an address is followed by a dinner prepared by the wives of the parishioners. This is the price paid for admission to an event which, until 1853 was attended only by male chauvinists and held in the local tavern.

The Connecticut meetinghouses of East Haddam, 1794, and Norwichtown, 1801, as well as Vermont's East Poultney Baptist church are credited, because of their similarity to Fillmore's two previously noted churches, to the firm of Riley and Fillmore.

But credit must also be given, at this point, to Asher Benjamin. A plate from his 1797 book, *A Country Builder's Assistant,* contains a clear copy of what must have been the origin of Fillmore's churches (see photo).

So much for pure creativity. The Palladian window, used extensively during the Federal Period, may be traced not only to Italy's Andrea Palladio, but to his predecessor, Serlio, who first introduced it under the name "Serliana." In architecture, plagiarism is a compliment rather than a crime. It is not even necessary to reveal one's sources since they are usually self-evident. But in this context it is unlikely that Serlio was aware that the earliest example of the first so-called "Palladian" design feature occurs in the House of Neptune in Herculaneum, and remained buried until the early eighteenth century.

Services: Sunday, 10 a.m.
Seating Capacity: 725
Open to visitors: Not open to visitors.
Telephone: (802) 388-7634
Construction Cost: $9000
How to get there: The church is located in the center of town, at the corner of Main, Pleasant and Seymour Streets, a quarter-mile from the Vermont tourist bus stop.

Architect: **Fillmore, Lavius** (see page 83).

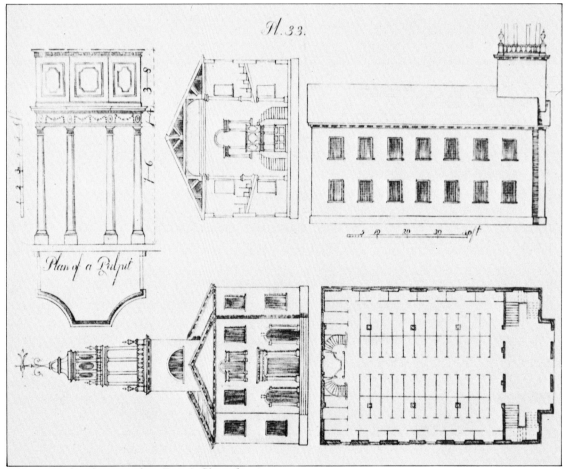

Asher Benjamin's Design For A Church

An ecumenical phenomenon

Round Church

Bridge Street, Richmond, Vermont 05477

Completed in 1813   **William Rhodes, builder**

The setting is vintage Vermont. Twelve miles east of Burlington lies a lush valley almost completely surrounded by receding mountain ranges, reminiscent of the valley of Gruyere in Switzerland. But instead of a feudal castle towering over its center, this valley is studded with numerous farms, each one proudly accented by clusters of gleaming aluminum silo domes in varying height and number.

In the center of the valley is the town of Richmond, current population circa 3000 (including an Olympic Gold Medalist) and the locale of the famous "Round Church." This remarkable structure is a modest, yet eloquent, response to man's subconscious desire for spiritual unity with his fellows. The geometry of its plan dates back to the fourth century A.D. when Santa Costanza in Rome, San Vitale in Ravenna and Charlemagne's Chapel in Aix-la-Chapelle gave legitimacy as well as lineage to an approach that was logical as well as liturgically correct.

Because of its structural limitations, the round form was abandoned a millennium ago in favor of the longitudinal plan. The processional, or "railroad" car effect, though it emphasized architectural grandeur as well as rigidity of doctrine, did little, however, for communications and acoustics. Precisely for these reasons, the central plan was revived with great enthusiasm in 1959, resulting in such striking creations as the circular Benedictine Priory in St. Louis and the vast elliptical underground basilica in Lourdes, France.

But these sophisticated structures, responding to Pope John's plea for Christian unity, *"Ut unum sint,"* were anticipated in Richmond, Vermont by a century and a half. All of them, furthermore, are strictly sectarian creations, while Richmond's central plan encompassed the full range of American Protestantism. The Richmond church was inspired by twenty-nine Congregationalists, twenty-one Universalists, five "Christians," five Baptists and a solitary Methodist. The Episcopalians, in 1812, were undoubtedly still occupied in their struggle to gain a foothold in the more populated areas of southern New England.

The land was donated by Thomas Whitcomb, a tavern keeper, and Isaac Gleason, a storekeeper. The building was erected by William

Round Church; Richmond, Vermont

Rhodes and seventeen experienced helpers for a total of approximately $3000. The town financed the building by the sale of pews.

The "Round Church" is not strictly round. It is hexkaidecagonal in plan, made up of sixteen ten-foot wide sections. It has three Greek-Revival entrances, in acknowledgment to the most up-to-date fire laws. Each section, except those in which the entrances occur, has two windows, providing evenly-balanced light and ventilation to the main floor as well as to the horseshoe-shaped gallery.

The Richmond church is not visually dramatic. But alongside the typical New England clapboard churches with their attached spires and porticoes, most of which owe servile allegiance to Sir James Gibbs, it is a refreshing and pleasant surprise. Parenthetically, the Shakers and the Quakers as well, adopted the functional circular plan for their barns, although they retained the rectangular plan for their houses of worship.

The Richmond Round Church is no longer a regular place of worship but a meetinghouse and a historic monument. It is superseded by two totally undistinguished uni-denominational rectangular structures near the town's center. But for him "that hath ears to hear," the voices of six generations of worshipers can still be heard echoing in the amphitheatrical Vermont setting of the famous "Round Church."

Services: Annual Pilgrimage, last Sunday in July.
Seating Capacity: 400
Open to visitors: 11 a.m. to 4 p.m., July 1 through Labor Day; during foliage season.
Telephone: Contact the Richmond Historical Society, Box 453, Richmond, Vermont 05477.
Construction Cost: Approximately $3000.
How to get there: From I-89, take exit 11 (Richmond). Drive on Route 2 to the center of Richmond Village. At the four corners, turn right onto Bridge Street. The church is on the left, just across the Winooski River, less than a mile from the center of the village.
Architect: Rhodes, William. Biography not available.

Saint Paul's Episcopal Cathedral

Cathedral of the Immaculate Conception

First Unitarian Universalist Church

The Burlington Triad

The desire to erect structures designed specifically for worship is as old as history. Perhaps the act of building a church is in itself a form of worship. If this is true, and according to Voltaire, equally true that, "If God did not exist, man would have to create Him," then it seems not unlikely that man might build churches partly out of sheer enthusiasm for architecture as an end in itself.

An incident in the New Testament may be used as an illustration. The gospels of Matthew, Mark and Luke each describe the episode referred to as "The Transfiguration" in which Christ appears suddenly clothed in radiant light. The disciple Peter, "not knowing what he said," is reported to have proposed to Christ, "Let us build here three tabernacles, one for thee, one for Moses, and one for Elias." A voice from the clouds was then heard to say, "This is my beloved son, hear ye him." This could be interpreted as a clear reminder to Peter, "the rock on which I will build my church," that the actual building of churches was the last thing that God and His son had in mind.

(It was certainly a lucky break for Peter. If he had acquainted himself with the plans and specifications for tabernacles as outlined in the Book of Exodus, he would have found out that a single church, and not three, would have been a whole life's work with no time off for spreading the gospel.)

In any case, since the early Christians emerged from the catacombs, some five million churches have been built throughout the world. In Burlington, the northwest reaches of Vermont, there are twelve. Three of them are outstanding and within walking distance from each other. They house radically different denominations, and their styles range from the red-brick-and-white-trim of the Federal Period to the Beton Brut of the immediate present.

First Unitarian Universalist Church; Burlington, Vermont

92

First Unitarian Universalist Church

141 Pearl Street, Burlington, Vermont 05401

Completed in December 1806   Peter Banner,
Charles Bulfinch, architects

The First Universalist Unitarian Church is a prim, stately redbrick ed-ifice with a white spire that dominates the north end of Church Street as regally as the cathedral at the apex of the Grand Boulevard in Reims. It is the city's oldest existing house of worship. The atmosphere of hushed respect that envelops this eminently attractive and obviously prosperous town seems in gratitude for the church's presence.

The structure was built in 1806 in the unbelievably short space of seven months. It was a town project; the bricks and shingles were made locally, and the stone was quarried in the city itself. Samuel Reed was the builder; the final bill was $12,185.32. Its design is attributed to Peter Banner, whose Park Street Church in Boston is reflected in the porches on either side of the tower. Receipts in the archives, signed by Charles Bulfinch as well as by Peter Banner, suggest that the design may have been the result of some form of collaboration.

The church was originally heated by two wood-burning stoves whose pipes ran exposed the full length of the interior. By a curious coincidence, Bulfinch's Unitarian Church in Lancaster, Massachusetts, still retains this same incongruous yet highly efficient feature. It is not known whether Bulfinch ignored its presence and condoned it as a nec-essary evil, or whether he embraced it wholeheartedly for its environ-mental value.

It is interesting to speculate on the image of the prosperous Boston-based architect traveling diagonally across the whole of New England with a roll of drawings protruding from his saddlebag. His fee, origina-ting among a congregation consisting of some fifty persons, must have been modest by any standards; the journey, even by the direct Concord-White River Junction-Montpelier route, must have taken at least ten days.

Historical precedents of traveling architects, however, are not lack-ing. William of Sens crossed the channel in the thirteenth century to de-sign Canterbury Cathedral. He eventually fell from the scaffolding and died for his efforts.

And none less than the flamboyant Gianlorenzo Bernini, with a retinue of some forty artisans and servants, traveled from Rome to Paris in 1665 with a design for the east facade of the Louvre which was summarily rejected by Colbert, Louis XIV's minister and architectural adviser.

Today's architect may travel by Volkswagen or by Lear Jet, but he must make the necessary house calls, regardless of the distance, if he wishes to retain control of the execution of his design.

So much for the pitfalls of the professional that is sometimes called the "mother of all the arts."

The pastors, too (who, at the option of the Society, might be paid in grain, beef, pork, butter or cheese), were not without their personal tribulations.

In Burlington in 1820, one Abigail Day publicly accused the pastor, Samuel Clark, of bribery and cheating the members of the Society "in an improper and unchristianlike manner." Abigail Day was summarily hustled out and, although the charge was never disproven, forced to join a neighboring congregation. This colorful event is prominently featured in church chronicles. It has never been made clear, however, whether she was ejected because she had the courage to speak out or because the congregation was already three-quarters female.

Another incident in Burlington concerns Joshua Young who was engaged as pastor in 1852 at an annual salary of $1000. He was well liked and respected by the congregation. But because he openly expressed his support for the abolitionist John Brown, he was forced to resign in 1863.

Evidently there was a strict dividing line between freedom of religion and freedom of expression.

Services: Sunday, 11 a.m., except in summer.
Seating Capacity: 450
Open to visitors: 8 a.m. to 12 noon, except in summer.
Telephone: (802) 862-8630
Construction Cost: $22,185
How to get there: The church is in the center of town, at the north end of Church Street, the town's main business street.

Architects: **Banner, Peter** (see page 23) and **Bulfinch, Charles** (see page 12).

Saint Paul's Episcopal Cathedral

1 Cathedral Square, Burlington, Vermont 05401

Completed in October 1973   Burlington Associates, Inc., architects

From the foot of Cherry Street, the view of Lake Champlain and the distant Adirondack Mountains beyond is spectacular. Seen from the opposite shore, man's own handiwork is hardly comparable.

But the ambience resulting from the juxtaposition of man and nature is well worth driving the length of Route Seven. Nature has contributed a site that must be the envy of every church architect; man has complemented it with a design that deserves the acclaim of this and all future generations.

St. Paul's Episcopal Cathedral Church, at first glance, resembles a rather self-conscious assemblage of abstract elements contrived primarily to catch the eye. And yet it looks like a church. There are, to be sure, no spires, no high arched windows, no flying buttresses. But there is a reminder of the Early Christian bell-tower, and the semi-circular opening over the entrance door immediately recalls the Romanesque tympanum.

It is sheathed neither in traditional stone nor in local brick or clapboard. Here to paraphrase the gospels, "the stone that the builders rejected" was replaced by contemporary concrete.

The choice can hardly be termed a breakthrough. Auguste Perret built the first all-concrete church in LeRaincy, France, in 1923. LeCorbusier immortalized "beton-brut" at Ronchamp in 1956; Marcel Breuer gave birth to the "Brutal Style" when he designed St. John's in Collegeville, Minnesota. Felix Candela exploited the fluidity and grace of his concrete shells in Mexico in the '60s, an approach that was climaxed by Pier Luigi Nervi in the Benedictine Priory in St. Louis.

And in 1973, the firm of Burlington Associates joined the galaxy of great names when, miraculously, they won a competition for a design of a church in their own city.

Their solution is worthy of the tradition of design that has distinguished ecclesiastical architecture for two millenia. The workmanship, too, matches the controlled surfaces that characterize the work of I. M. Pei in the east wing of Washington's National Gallery.

Burlington's St. Paul's is without a doubt one of the most handsome

Saint Paul's Episcopal Cathedral; Burlington, Vermont

contemporary cathedrals.

Like Le Corbusier's Chapel, it can be enjoyed from all sides. Much has already been said about the full utilization of the site, and the happy inclusion of a sheltered garden near the main entrance. Less has been recorded, however, about the slight southerly slope of the site. Here the architect, to the rapturous acclaim of generations of mothers, has placed the lower level nursery entrance immediately accessible to the parking area.

A detailed appraisal of the floor plan reveals nothing startling or original. The sanctuary is essentially a simple block over which the coffered ceiling seems to hover protectively. But the ensemble, seen during a service, is intensely stimulating. No stained glass can match the magnificent view that accompanies the sun through the full-height south window; no medieval tapestry can compare with the unique wood sculpture on the opposite wall that makes a virtue of the air conditioning grilles.

When the red-robed choir adds sound and harmony to form, texture and light, the whole becomes an unforgettable sensual experience. It achieves the ultimate aim of art by arousing a universal feeling of pleasure.

The present edifice replaces an undistinguished pseudo-Gothic structure designed by Ammi Young in 1831, destroyed by fire in 1971.

96

There is tension in reinforced concrete, translucency in plate glass, rhythm in lines, planes and solids.

This incident is commemorated in the cross over the altar, which is fashioned from nails salvaged from the ashes. A similar feature may be seen in the courtyard of Coventry Cathedral in England, where the fourteenth century church was the victim of enemy bombing in 1941.

In Burlington, so that "the gates of hell shall not prevail" against the new edifice, St. Paul's Cathedral Church has been fully fireproofed.

Services: Sunday, 8 and 10 a.m., 5:30 p.m.; Daily, 7 and 9 a.m.; Tuesday, Wednesday, 5:30 p.m.; Thursday, 10 a.m.; Holy Days, 10 a.m.

Seating Capacity: 500

Telephone: (802) 864-0471

Construction Cost: $1.6 million

Open to visitors: Monday to Friday, 9 a.m. to 4 p.m.; Saturday, 9 a.m. to 12 noon; Sunday, 7 a.m. to 12 noon; 5 to 6:30 p.m.

How to get there: Follow Vermont I-89 to Route 2 West. Go to the end of Main Street, then turn right onto Battery Street. Take the second left onto Cherry Street.

Architect: **Scullins, Thomas V.** Born in 1942, he was educated at Syracuse University and at Harvard. He is now associated with the firm of Alexander Treux de Groot Cullins, Inc., in Burlington, Vermont.

Architect: **Henderson, William.** Born in 1935, he was educated at Harvard University and is now practicing in Florida.

**Cathedral of the
Immaculate Conception;
Burlington, Vermont**

Light, space, proportion,
and symbolism provide
a powerful composition.

Cathedral of the Immaculate Conception

Pine Street, Burlington, Vermont 05401

Completed in 1977   **Edward L. Barnes, architect**

On the night of March 14, 1972, Burlington's 104-year-old Roman Catholic Cathedral of the Immaculate Conception was destroyed by a fire allegedly set by a former altar boy.

Exactly five years later a new cathedral was dedicated on the same site, completing the Burlington triad. The new Roman Catholic Cathedral is a highly provocative structure. The architect, Edward Larabee Barnes of New York, selected from a roster of 54 architects, has consciously cast aside any resemblance to its undistinguished Neo-Gothic predecessor, and created a new landmark in the Vermont panorama. The soaring profile in grey granite has been replaced by a tent-like structure sheathed in copper, resting on a low wall of green and brown glazed brick. The free standing bell-tower in Corten steel is a sculptural abstraction, recalling on a modest scale, the symbolism of the Carillon Tower of Stamford's First Presbyterian Church and Marcel Breuer's powerful "Bell Banner" in Collegeville, Minnesota.

The interior is not dark and mysterious, but white, bright, and filled with the western light that enters through a clerestory window recalling the Greek Cross.

Like its immediate neighbor to the west, St. Paul's Episcopal Cathedral (which, by a remarkable coincidence, rose from the ashes of its predecessor in the previous year), the new Roman Catholic Cathedral makes a powerful religious statement.

Both churches express the diversities in ritual that have been made legitimate (though somewhat begrudgingly, to be sure) since the Reformation.

This is an invitation to architectural originality that has been only recently acknowledged. Despite myriad interpretations of the Christian liturgy, their architectural enclosures, (until the last half of this century), have been imprisoned within the limited range of the historic styles.

Although there are over 250 Christian denominations in the United States, only recently has the architect dared to reach beyond the Byzantine, the Romanesque, the Gothic and the Baroque, to provide their respective shelters. Most surprisingly is the fact that rather than add the Rococo to his palette, the architect relegated this exuberant style to the moving-picture houses and turned inward to the pagan and liturgically irrelevant Neo-Classic.

Today's religious architecture, however, is bursting with promise. And perhaps this is what the Holy Spirit had in mind all along.

If architecture is indeed the "statement" that its practitioners claim, then it is a legitimate form of expression, and it deserves to be included among the "tongues" which are listed among the nine gifts of the Holy Spirit. And the languages implied were surely never intended to be in a limited list of dialects. Even the Apostles who turned linguists in a single instant were not restricted to Parthian, Median, Elamite, Cretan, Arabic, and the few tongues mentioned in the Acts of the Apostles. And if worship may be expressed in a variety of tongues, why not the building that encloses and declares their message?

Today's ecclesiastical architecture may be a belated response to this possibility. Surely no deity worthy of the name would be properly propitiated with a monotonous repetition of former habitations, despite the strict rules regarding the construction of the Temple in the Old Testament.

I much prefer the "many mansions" of the New Testament (a popular quotation whose significance I can grasp only in its obvious architectural connotation). What omnipotent deity deserves less than the newest, the best, the most inspired mansion that man could devise?

In this regard, the most profane thought comes to my mind. Could the Holy Spirit Himself, with His tongues of flame, have helped to set those fires?

Services: Monday to Friday, 7 a.m., 12:00 p.m.; Saturday, 4 and 5:30 p.m.; Sunday, 7:30, 9:30 and 11:30 a.m., and 12:30 p.m.

Open to visitors: Monday to Friday, 9 a.m. to 5 p.m.

Seating Capacity: 400, plus 250 in vestibule.

Telephone: (802) 658-4333

Construction Cost: Not available.

How to get there: Go north on Church Street (Burlington's main thoroughfare), to the end. Turn left onto Pearl Street, then take the second left onto Pine Street.

Architect: **Barnes, Edward Larabee,** FAIA.
Born in Chicago, Illinois in 1915. Barnes was educated at Harvard University, BS, Cum Laude and M. Arch. 1942. Present Firm: Edward Larabee Barnes Associates, New York, New York. Work represented: Cathedral Church of the Immaculate Conception, Burlington, Vermont. Other important works: Projects throughout New England, New York and the Midwest, in the academic, religious and commercial fields, as well as museums and centers for the performing arts and master planning. He received numerous local and national awards and citations, notably the 1972 Louis Sullivan Award for Architecture and the American Institute of Architects Firm Award in 1980.

Charterhouse of the Transfiguration
Skyline Drive, Mount Equinox, Arlington, Vermont 05250

Completed in 1970   **Victor Christ-Janer, architect**

Architecture is a visual art. Buildings are made to be used, but they are almost invariably built to be seen as well. Few great buildings exist, in fact, that were not purposely erected to honor and flatter their creators.

The exceptions are extremely rare. There is one in Spain, in the northern Pyrenees. In the twelfth century a small group of religious persons built the monastery of San Juan de la Pena under an overhanging cliff about eighteen miles from the town of Jaca. The cloister is a jewel of Spanish Romanesque architecture; the carved capitals, depicting successive episodes in the life of Christ, are breathtaking in their simple beauty.

But this monastery was not built to be seen and admired. It was an act of total dedication by a group of spiritually oriented souls who chose to do the Lord's work, as they saw it, removed from the stream of everyday life. They could not possibly have dreamed that their remote habitation would someday become an architectural shrine.

Another example, equally rare, is to be found on the slopes of Mount Equinox in Vermont. It is the Charterhouse of the Transfiguration, the only center of the Carthusian Order in America. The community consists of some fifteen Fathers and Brothers who, in addition to espousing lives of poverty, chastity and obedience, have elected to devote themselves fully to the service of God and of mankind through solitude and silence. They, too, have detached themselves from the outside world and reside in an atmosphere of complete isolation.

Needless to say, their self-imposed way of life presented a difficult problem for their architect. Their habitation must be directed inward, not outward. It must serve the chapter and its members only and not invite intercourse with the general public. It was essential, above all else, to avoid the architectural expression of grandeur and human pride that, with rare exceptions, has been the mark of religious architecture throughout the ages.

The solution is a stroke of near-genius. Victor Christ-Janer, a gifted and sensitive Connecticut architect, has devised a community center that is an eloquent response to the full requirements of the program.

101

Charterhouse of the Transfiguration; Arlington, Vermont

The entire structure is enclosed with rough-hewn granite slabs, split at the quarry in Barre, and left unfinished. These dolmen-like wall sections, measuring nine and a half feet by three and a half feet by thirteen inches thick and weighing three and a half tons, are held in place at the top by a continuous reinforced concrete lintel. The resulting effect is one of great inner strength, unfailing integrity, utter simplicity and evokes nothing in the viewer so much as reverent silence.

And yet the rough, almost forbidding texture of the mute and solemn slabs is relieved throughout by the marks of drill-rods that seem to caress their edges like the fingers of numberless nameless workmen. This persistent note adds a human touch to a building that is a monument to its own intrinsic anonymity.

The term "Charterhouse" is derived from Chartreuse, a range of mountains near Grenoble in France. It was in the nearby area known as Cartusium that Saint Bruno founded the Order of Carthusians in 1085. The Vermont Charterhouse was completed in 1970. It is visible only from the Skyline drive, at a point about a mile distant. Visitors to the Charterhouse itself are not permitted; although the edifice is acknowledged as an architectural *succes d'estime,* architects, too, are sternly discouraged. For the present, it is a private dialogue in stone and does not encourage eavesdropping. The message of its architecture is not phrased for the transient, restless outside world.

Services: Not open to the public.   **Open to visitors:** Not open to visitors.
Seating Capacity: Unknown.   **Telephone:** (802) 362-2550
Construction Cost: Unknown.

How to get there: The Charterhouse may be viewed only from Skyline Drive. Inquire at the Gatehouse at the start of the Drive.

Architect: **Christ-Janer, Victor**, AIA. Born in Waterville, Minnesota in 1911. Christ-Janer was educated at Lake Erie College, AFD and Yale University, BFA and B. Arch. Present Firm: Victor Christ-Janer & Associates. Work represented: Cathusian Charterhouse, Arlington, Vermont. Other important works: St. Mary's Abbey, Morristown, New Jersey and Central New York Psychiatric Center, Syracuse, New York.

New Hampshire

The state of New Hampshire contains a wealth of churches that, for reasons not entirely clear, have not been properly publicized.

Perhaps it is because though many of us think little of traveling from Boston to New York and returning the same day, New Hampshire seems rather remote.

And yet it must not have seemed remote two centuries ago, when numberless, nameless, but intensely hardy souls traveled there, by horse and on foot, to build more churches in proportion to the population than in any of the other New England states.

It must be that inspiration and imagination, and not minutes and miles, are the true dimensions of time and space. Were it not for this, we would probably all still be living in the Dark Ages, and all the great churches in the Western world would never have been erected.

Union Episcopal Church; Claremont, New Hampshire

Union Episcopal Church

Old Church Road, Claremont, New Hampshire 03743

Completed in 1771   **Ebenezer Wright, builder**

Claremont, in New Hampshire's southwest quadrant, is a self-sufficient microcosm of some 16,000 inhabitants who are involved in the same diurnal and nocturnal preoccupations as the rest of the nation. They have found the time and the devotion, however, to build a miniscule galaxy of no less than fifteen churches, all within the town's limits.

The result is a melange that includes few surprises. There is a Baptist, a Congregational, a Lutheran, a Methodist church, and there are two Roman Catholic churches. There is also a Greek Orthodox church with its "onion domes" silhouetted against the sky. And the Episcopalians have provided a fascinating example of "Board-and-Batten" Gothic whose exposed wood framing of a century past recalls the steel diagonals that distinguish Chicago's John Hancock Building of this decade. Each of these buildings is in constant competition with the town's secular architecture, and none is sufficiently distinctive to merit special consideration.

A single structure has escaped the inexorable juggernaut of what is commonly termed progress. The Union Episcopal Church, two miles from the town's epicenter, has mercifully been bypassed by the arteries of traffic that keep the town alive and prosperous, and now stands alone in a setting that, except for the graveyard, has changed little since the church was erected.

In 1764 a group of Episcopalians emigrated from Farmington, Connecticut on snowshoes (so the legend goes) and laid out the 25 "rights" of land that they had purchased. The rights, or shares, consisted of 320 acres.

In 1773 they completed the erection of the present church. According to the record, the plans were furnished by Governor John Wentworth, and the erection was carried out under the direction of master carpenter Ichabod Hitchcock. No one knows what the "plans" consisted of, but by coincidence the present building follows the general plan of the Congregational church in Farmington, and resembles, more closely, the church in Brooklyn, also in Connecticut. How the Governor obtained these "plans" or what they consisted of as actual useful documents will never be known because useful building plans, except those drawn up and promulgated by Asher Benjamin in his book *"The Country Builder's Assistant,"* were practically nonexistent. (It should be noted that the Farmington and the Brooklyn churches were completed in 1771, just two years before Union Church.)

The interior is furnished with the usual strangely uncomfortable "box pews" which were sold individually to help finance construction. This type of seating is often referred to as "sheep-pen" pews. I wonder if this appellation is an indirect reference to Christ's admonition to Peter, "Feed my sheep?"

The interior is adorned by a reproduction, in leaded-glass, of the painting "Light of the World" by the Pre-Raphaelite English painter William Holman Hunt which was donated to the church in 1875.

An unusual event occurred a generation after the erection of the church. In 1817 Virgil Barber, son of Union Church's third minister, Daniel Barber, left his wife and five daughters and became a Roman Catholic priest. In 1823 he bought the land across from Old Church Road and erected St. Mary's, the first Roman Catholic church in New Hampshire.

The odd-looking structure is no longer in use. But both churches seem to enjoy their juxtaposition. Together they represent a gentle statement, if not in favor of ecumenism, at least in acknowledgement of the First Amendment to the Constitution. And on Christmas Eve, during the Candlelight Service, the facades of both churches are lighted up by the same fires, and echo the sounds of the same carols.

Services: Sunday, 9 a.m.
Seating Capacity: 350
Open to visitors: By appointment.
Telephone: (603) 542-6553
Construction Cost: Unknown.
How to get there: Go south toward Charlestown on Route 11. Turn right at the third traffic light, and right again at the Old Railroad Station. Continue north on Old Church Road for one-half mile. Union Church is on the right.

Architect: **Unknown.**

First Church, Unitarian

Main Street, Peterborough, New Hampshire 03458

Completed in 1825   **Architect Unknown**

Sir Banister Fletcher, the noted architectural historian, describes Peterborough's principal monument, in part, as " . . . a grand western facade, with three gigantic arches." He is referring, however, to the 12th century cathedral in Peterborough, England, and not to the early 19th century church in Peterborough, New Hampshire. But the coincidence is nonetheless pleasing.

The facade of the Unitarian Church is also distinguished by three arches. And there are other parallels. In each case, the name of the original architect is not known. And the problem of tracking them down is no less fascinating in New England than it is in medieval Europe.

This history of the design of Peterborough's First Unitarian Church is a curious web of events laced with probabilities and assumptions. The building committee allegedly acquired a set of plans from an associate in Charles Bulfinch's office while he was away. The plans were presumed to have been made originally for Lancaster's Unitarian Church, but rejected because they lacked the necessary seating capacity.

Since the Lancaster Church was completed in 1816, the plans must have lain about for a musty decade, because, although the record states that on April 20, 1816 the Selectmen voted " . . . to see if the town will build a new meetinghouse," Peterborough's church was not completed until 1825.

Bulfinch meanwhile allegedly played a part, along with Peter Banner of Boston, in the design of the Unitarian Church in Burlington, Vermont, also completed in 1816! A busy year not only for the Unitarians, but for Bulfinch, who had numerous secular projects "on the boards," at the time, not the least of which was the completion of the Capitol in Washington.

Meanwhile, the Newport Congregational Church appeared in 1823 to cloud the issue. It was erected by John Leach, builder, but it contains some obvious Bulfinch touches. One is "the gigantic arches" in recessed brick that articulate the facade, just as they do in Peterborough. Another is the continuous cornice that binds the entire composition, just as it does in Lancaster. And a third is the projecting porch that seems to

First Church, Unitarian; Peterborough, New Hampshire

PETERBOROUGH, NEW HAMPSHIRE

belong somewhere between Peterborough's plain end wall, without the porch, and the imposing portico that distinguishes the Lancaster church. To add to the confusion, the steeple of Newport's church repeats the detail of the church in Acworth, fifteen miles to the south, while the main body of the church is exactly like that of Deerfield, Massachusetts, built, not before, but a year later!

And finally, the belfry of the wooden church in Chester, Vermont, built in 1828, repeats in detail the one that sets astride the church in Peterborough. Sinnott surmises that the builder (in this case, unknown) passing from Boston to Chester, admired the Peterborough belfry and resolved to copy it. But what was he doing in Boston? Combing through Bulfinch's rejected plans, perhaps?

If we are able to untangle this Gordian knot, we should be well prepared to attack the problem of Peterborough Cathedral in England. Indeed, perhaps the secret is to be found in Peterborough, New Hampshire, where the second Unitarian minister, Dr. Abiel Abbot, established the world's first tax-supported Free Public Library.

Services: Sunday, 10:45 a.m.
Open to visitors: 9 a.m. to 1 p.m. (except in summer) and by appointment.
Seating Capacity: 450
Telephone: (603) 924-6245
Construction Cost: $6,140.69
How to get there: The town of Peterborough is on Route 101, roughly halfway between Nashua and Keene, where Route 101 is crossed by Route 202. The church is in the center of town, near the northwest corner of Summer Street.

Architect:**Unknown.**

Maine, State of Serendipity

Until recently the State of Maine, to me, was no more than a vast forest of evergreens edged with fishing villages, a seasonal retreat heavily flavored with chanterelles, lobster, and blueberries, and scented to near-intoxication with its special bracing atmosphere. And a state of presidential primaries with its own native accent.

But I have discovered that it is an architectural historian's gold mine. Its southern periphery alone (which isn't all that far away once you get there) has added two huge nuggets to history's list of important houses of worship.

Modesty, simplicity, sincerity, and a touch of grandeur

Alna Meetinghouse
RFD #1, Route 128, Wiscasset, Maine 04578

Completed in 1804   **Joseph Carleton, builder**

This late Colonial meetinghouse, in a setting of broad valleys and wooded hills, resembles a lonesome, bewildered ghost. It is all that remains of what must once have been a devout and thriving community. Except for the fact that it has no proper chimney, Alna Meetinghouse might be taken for a farmhouse.

Actually it is a typical early New England house of worship, with gable ends instead of the usual hip roof. Dwarfed by its context, it is relatively unimpressive.

But its interior is a glory of American architcture. Like Hingham's Old Ship Meetinghouse, which it resembles, it is haunted to overflowing with the spirits of all those who built it and worshiped there, like the innumerable figures crowded into a medieval tapestry.

Immediately upon entering, one can identify them by their works. Present are the solemn elders who approved its fifty-foot eight-inch by forty-foot seven-inch dimensions and sited it facing west, just like Chartres Cathedral. Here are the woodsmen who felled the chestnut trees and hewed the giant beams that assure its solidity.

Close by are the teams of sawyer and pitman who provided the twenty-inch-wide by twenty-foot-long floorboards. On one side is the master carpenter who marked out the box-pews in the gallery as well as on the main floor; on the other is the artisan who turned the spindles that decorate their top rails and the nameless craftsman who, in this modest Protestant ensemble, imposed a magnificent Baroque pulpit. And finally, the unsung genius who, in deference to the first minister (who must have been unusually short), devised a platform that could be adjusted to preachers of different heights.

What hours, what days of individual dedication, what weekends of group organization to make tangible and permanent the faith of this miniscule society! What snatches of conversation, what fiery sermons, what hymns and "lined-out" psalms still echo in this beautifully preserved, unrestored interior. Did they dream, I wonder, that their combined selfless efforts, many miles from nowhere, would one day be immortalized on the National Register of Historic Places?

Alna Meetinghouse; Wiscasset, Maine

Built far off the beaten path by anonymous believers, this is a lasting and eloquent monument to faith, "the substance of things hoped for, the evidence of things not seen." (Hebrews 5, 14)

As I was studying the exterior, I heard human voices. At the rear of the building two workmen were removing the rounded, natural stones that had fallen away from their original settings in the foundation. They showed me, with a mixture of modesty and pride, how they were replacing them with new cut stones three times the size of the originals. And it occurred to me that, in all my New England peregrinations, I had never encountered such gigantic effort, by hand, combined with such skill and love.

They were unquestionably descendants of the men and women who had erected the meetinghouse almost two centuries ago. I wonder if this phenomenon, so rare in our time, is to be found only in the demanding soil and rewarding atmosphere of Maine?

I wonder too, if tomorrow's archeologists will measure today's computer-designed, machine-produced, air-conditioned houses of praise by the same standards that establish such a high value on the works of the past?

Services: None.
Seating Capacity: 400
Open to visitors: By appointment with Clifton Walker, caretaker.
Telephone: (207) 586-5951
Construction cost: Unknown.
How to get there: Take Route 218 north from Wiscasset for seven miles.

Architect: **Unknown.**

First Parish Church; Brunswick, Maine

First Parish Church
9 Cleaveland Street, Brunswick, Maine 04011

Completed in December 1845   **Richard Upjohn, architect**
                                                   Coombs & Graves, builder

Maine's second architectural treasure is the First Parish Church in
Brunswick. Its official designation is the United Church of Christ. Located at the intersection of Maine Street and Routes 24 and 123, it marks
the principal approach to Bowdoin College. You can't miss it! (Although
I did. When I asked a quintet of unisexed teenagers for "The Upjohn
Church," they directed me to St. Paul's Episcopal Church on Pleasant
Avenue.) St. Paul's Church although it antedates First Parish, is of passing interest only. First Parish, on the other hand, is of national significance. It is the paradigm of the "Board-and-Batten" style that within
two decades spread throughout the entire United States.

First Parish was erected by Coolidge Graves and Isaiah Coombs at a
total cost of $13,101. It was dedicated on March 18, 1846, two months
prior to the consecration of its better-known counterpart, Trinity Episcopal in downtown New York. Most surprising is the fact that both of
these influential structures were designed by the same architect.

Their simultaneous appearance sparked two parallel trends, one in
masonry and one in wood, that lasted a full half-century. It is of these
movements that Pierson writes, "St. Patrick's (in stone) spoke of the
growing strength and size of the nation's institutions, while the small
wooden church spoke of the vitality of America's middle-class towns and
villages." Both these trends can be traced directly to the energy and genius of Richard Upjohn.

English-born Richard Upjohn is credited with the design of almost
one hundred churches throughout the Eastern states. In Brunswick's
First Parish, his most notable work in New England, he achieved a double *tour de force.* First of all, he conceived the all-wood Gothic church
which survives today as a unique and pervasive element in the American scene.

And secondly, in his first non-Episcopalian design, he broke the
century-old tradition of neo-Classic design and devised a style that was
welcomed by all denominations. Upjohn's Gothic influence was as widespread and as durable as that of his flamboyant successor Henry Hobson Richardson with his Romanesque style.

Upjohn's all-wood church with its steep pitched roof and pointed-arch opening was adopted without hesitation by the loyal Episcopalians. It was adopted also by the Roman Catholics in Georgetown, Connecticut, the Unitarians in Charleston, South Carolina, the Presbyterians in Fairplay, Colorado, and the Baptists in Plains, Georgia. The first church that I attended, in fact, was a tiny Board-and-Batten Irvingite Chapel in Clifton Heights, Missouri.

At first glance, First Parish hardly rivals Wells Cathedral in England, with its park-like setting, or Ulm Cathedral, in southern Germany, with its 529-foot spire. Its prime and only misfortune, however, is that it is squeezed mercilessly within a busy triple intersection. Its setting does justice neither to the church nor to the college of which it is the symbol. Nevertheless, it is a handsome and imposing structure, pure Gothic in mass and in detail. The same principles that were expressed with power and grace in the ribbed vaults, the flying buttresses, and pointed arches of medieval architecture in stone have been transposed, in the hands of a master, into wood.

In the tradition of the medieval *maitres d'oeuvres*, Upjohn respected the exigencies of the local material and adapted them to the Congregational ritual. Vitruvius, with his three basic precepts "Firmness, Commodity, and Delight," would have heartily approved the results. And if the French chronicler Villard de Honnecourt and the English Master-Mason Henry Yevele (who is closely associated with Canterbury Cathedral and Westminster Abbey) are turning over in their graves, it can only be in order to get a better look!

The interior evokes a thesaurus of contradictions. At first glance it is a confusing assemblage of meaningless woodwork. But it is also a dramatic stage-set for a miracle-play. It appears to be a self-conscious montage of derivative forms and shapes. And yet it is actually a triumph of hammer-beam construction.

The focal point of the interior is, of course, the spectacular roof system. It is a principle devised in medieval England to lighten the roof load, and which culminated in many dazzling displays of structural vertuosity. The best known example is Great Hall in Westminster Palace in London. As reflected here, it is simply ravishing. It is a breathtaking example of what can be done in wood to match thrust with counterthrust, to balance tension and compression, and to create a ceiling that is as beautiful as it is structurally sound. That, of course, is what Gothic architecture in stone was all about in the first place.

The whole is a structural work of art, as reassuring as the hull of a ship, as intriguing as a spider's web, and as thrilling as a suspension bridge. And as I compare First Parish with its famous prototype, I find the Westminster Hall Palace ceiling heavy and pretentious. The spoilsport purists may maintain that a particular form cannot be transposed from one material to another without a noticeable loss of integrity. They deserve to be reminded, however, that the Greek temples that we know in translucent Pentellic marble are stylized developments from original

The interior is one of definitive perfection, the epitome of ingenuity in roof construction in wood. But if Jonathan Edwards had delivered his sermon, "Sinners in the hands of an angry God" here (delivered in Enfield, in 1741), would he have been remembered?

columns and beams in wood.

And curiously enough, the same sacred forms in marble were transposed back into wood when our early nineteenth century builders found it more convenient to utilize the native New England timber rather than Sir James Gibbs' London stone. I am tempted to quote the old chestnut, *"Plus ca change, plus c'est la même chose!"*

The structure of praise is not limited to the art of building. When I last visited First Parish, a string trio, which included a beautiful Japanese violinist, was in rehearsal. The delicate intricate harmonies seemed a perfect complement to the inspired interior.

I recalled a similar incident when a friend took me up a stone spiral stair to the choir loft in Paris' Notre Dame, and we heard Marcel Dupre play a thundering mass on the great eighteenth-century organ.

Except for an understandable difference in reverberation time, the two incidents were not dissimilar. Johann Sebastian Bach would have noted the obvious parallels as well as the contrasts. Notre Dame in Paris is a Mass, a requiem, a full symphony; First Parish, with its rhythmic repetition of resilient hammer-beams and arches, is a fugue or a passacaglia.

It occurs to me, too, that Goethe who is credited with the phrase,

"Architecture is frozen music" might at this very moment be lending an approving ear to the sounds that filled this magnificent instrument. But I have always wondered, why "frozen"? Well, in the context of Maine's ferocious winters, maybe Goethe was right!

The parallels between Brunswick's First Parish Church and Providence's First Baptist Meetinghouse are intriguing. Both designs were the result of powerful European influences, a century apart. English-born Upjohn carried on the Gothic Revival after his association with French-born English architect Augustus Welby Pugin. Providence's church shows the direct influence of London's James Gibbs.

Both designs sparked a distinctive architectural style. First Baptist was the origin of the Federal Style that swept the New England region. Brunswick's church was the springboard for the wooden "Board-and-Batten" Gothic that spread throughout the entire country in the late 1800s.

And both architects were successful authors. Gibbs with *A Book of Architecture* published in 1726, and Upjohn with *Upjohn's Rural Architecture with Designs, Working Drawings, and Specifications for a Rural Church.*

Both structures were designed to accommodate commencement exercises, First Parish for Bowdoin College and First Baptist for Brown University. And both, to be sure, are listed on the National Register of Historic Places.

But the similarities are not endless. The 185-foot Gibbs-inspired spire of Providence's meetinghouse, "though it swayed and bent," survived the Great Gale of 1813 as well as the destructive hurricane of 1938. Brunswick's Gothic *flèche* was destroyed by a nameless "gale" on October 30, 1866 and never replaced.

Services: Sunday, 10 a.m.
Open to visitors: Monday to Friday, 9 a.m. to 4 p.m.; Summers, Monday to Friday, 9 a.m. to 12 noon.
Seating Capacity: 800
Telephone: (207) 725-2172
Construction Cost: "Somewhat over $13,000."
How to get there: As you enter Brunswick from Pleasant Street, continue straight ahead to Main Street. Turn right, and two blocks on the left is First Parish Church.

Architect: **Upjohn, Richard.** 1802-1878. Born in Shattesbury, Dorsen, England. Education: Apprentice to a builder and cabinet-maker. Upjohn emigrated to America in 1828 and established offices first in New Bedford then in 1833 in Boston, and in 1853 in New York with his son, Richard Mitchell Upjohn. Work represented: First Parish Church, Brunswick, Maine. Upjohn introduced a form of English Gothic to America and designed many outstanding churches throughout New England and New York including Trinity Episcopal Church and St. Thomas Episcopal Church in New York City. He also designed several banks, libraries, and many private residences. He was founder and first president of the American Institute of Architects, and an honorary member of the Royal Institute of British Architects and the Institute of Portuguese Architects.

Rhode Island

Rhode Island boasts a series of superlative religious structures that encircle the state like an ecumenical chaplet. Within a circuit of less than fifty miles, six denominations are represented by eight outstanding buildings, five of which qualify as either the oldest, the most unusual or the most beautiful in their respective categories.

Start in Newport, naturally. Why? Because the town itself, along with Boston and New Haven, is one of New England's superior architectural attractions. Don't try to avoid being seduced by the town's magnificent mansions. See a half dozen or so of its hundred-odd, and get them into your system, not out. In this way you will be able all the better to savour the unique contrast between the voluptuous exuberance of the late nineteenth-century residences and the dignified reserve of its eighteenth-century houses of worship. You will find out that, unlike Ulysses, you will not be threatened with shipwreck by the siren symphony emanating from the breakers, nor will you be turned into pigs. You will simply develop a healthy, educated appetite for more of the town's many architectural treasures.

Trinity Episcopal Church; Newport, Rhode Island

The stamp of Wren with a pre-Revolutionary postmark

Trinity Episcopal Church
Queen Anne Square, Newport, Rhode Island 02840

Completed in September 1726   **Richard Munday, builder**

Of Newport's nineteen churches, two of them are treasures indeed. The first, Trinity Episcopal Church, was erected in 1726 by Master Carpenter Richard Munday. The spire is considered to be one of the loveliest in all of New England. According to the architectural historian, John Wedda and others, Sir Christopher Wren may have drawn the plans from which Richard Munday worked. This is not inconceivable, but in any case the descendance is not direct. Trinity's spire does resemble that of St. Lawrence Jewry in London, but it also reflects the design of the spire of William Price's Old North Church (now Christ Church) in Boston, which was completed three years previously. And William Price, print dealer and gentleman-architect, who is credited with the design of Old North, was one of the sponsors of Newport's Trinity. His professional connections may well account for the resemblance to Wren's work. The proportions of the towers of both Trinity and Old North are reflections of those of Wren's St. James Garlickhythe in London.

The evidence here of flattery's most sincere form is characteristic of all of architecture. Plagiarism, as we have said before, is not a crime in architecture, but a form of compliment, especially if the result does justice to the original.

Services: Sunday, 8 and 11 a.m. (10 a.m. in summer); Wednesday, 11 a.m.; Thursday, 12 noon.
Open to visitors: Summer, daily, 10 a.m. to 4 p.m.; otherwise by appointment.
Seating Capacity: 650
Telephone: (401) 846-0660
Construction Cost: 2000 pounds Sterling ($4400)
How to get there: Ask for Queen Anne Square. It is not far from the waterfront in the town's Historic District.

Architect: **Munday, Richard,** carpenter-builder. Native of Rhode Island. At one time he was associated with Benjamin Wyatt in planning and building houses, but later worked alone. He is best known for the design of Newport's Trinity Church. His outstanding achievement was Newport's Colony House, completed in 1725. He died in 1739.

Touro Synagogue; Newport, Rhode Island

Freedom of religion framed in freedom of expression

Touro Synagogue

85 Touro Street, Newport, Rhode Island 02840

Completed on December 2, 1763   **Peter Harrison, architect**

Newport's second religious jewel is Colonial America's oldest existing Jewish house of worship. (The first was built in New York.) The Sephardic Jews came to Newport in 1658. A century later, a group gathered under the leadership of Isaac Touro, newly arrived from the Rabbinical Academy of Amsterdam. They selected Peter Harrison, whom the architectural historian William Pierson refers to as "the very epitome of the gentleman-amateur," to design their new temple.

Having no traditional forms to adhere to, Harrison referred to several well-known book sources and combined them with Rabbi Touro's recommendations. The resulting structure, completed in 1763, is a Hebrew synagogue within a distinctly Georgian frame. According to Pierson, "the interior is many times more appropriate to the elegant dialogue of a

The artisans who worked on the Old Testament tabernacle, as described in detail in the book of Exodus, would be impressed, perhaps even delighted.

Restoration comedy than to the dark brooding intonement of the Hebrew service." Nevertheless, though not entirely flawless, the cubical meetinghouse volume is liturgically correct. Even the typically New England gallery serves a special denominational purpose: it is reserved for women. In this usage, the gallery corresponds to the second floor *gynaeceum* in Santa Sophia in Constantinople, to which women worshipers were relegated. The architectural commentary on equal rights, reverberating through the centuries, is obvious.

Civil rights, on the other hand, fare better in this context. Years before the promulgation of the Bill of Rights, George Washington granted full freedom of worship to Newport's Jewish inhabitants. The substantiating letter might also be listed among Newport's "firsts."

Services: June to Labor Day, Friday, 7:30 p.m.; rest of the year, 15 minutes before sunset; Saturday, 9 a.m.
Open to visitors: Sunday to Friday, end of June to September, 10 a.m. to 5 p.m.
Seating Capacity: 250
Telephone: (401) 847-4794
Construction Cost: Unknown.
How to get there: Ask for Touro Street in Newport's Historic District.

Architect: **Harrison, Peter** (see page 20).

The first Baptist church in America

First Baptist Church
75 North Main Street, Providence, Rhode Island 02903

Completed on May 27, 1775   **Joseph Brown, architect**
James Sumner, builder

Providence's principal historic monument literally sparkles with super-latives. The inscription on the 2500-pound bronze bell in its steeple reads, "The first Church in Rhode Island and the First Baptist Church in America." The steeple itself was the highest in New England until the twentieth century.

Providence's landmark was also the first to introduce the architecture of Sir James Gibbs to New England (Designs derived from his well-publicized *Book of Architecture*, published in 1728, had already appeared in Philadelphia's Christ Church in 1751 and in St. Michael's Church in Charleston, completed in 1752). Most important of all, Providence's landmark is the prime religious symbol of the state which, according to the official church brochure, "stands as the first in world history to establish civil liberty as its cornerstone."

Oddly enough, Roger Williams, who founded the state of Rhode Island and the American Baptist community, never saw the inside of a Baptist church. The Welsh-born graduate of Cambridge preached for almost a half century in private homes until he died in 1683.

The original Baptist structure was built in 1700, the second in 1726. The present one was the product of a minuscule congregation of one hundred eighteen worshipers who assembled in 1774 "to attend to, and to revive the affair of building a Meeting House, for the Publick worship of God, and also for holding Commencement in." The terminating phrase, with its odd grammatical liberties, was not an afterthought. It was a definite recognition of the dual purpose of the building and its close association with secular education.

The four Brown brothers, Nicholas, Joseph, John and Moses, were members of a wealthy merchant family. Joseph was a merchant, mathematician, astronomer and gentleman-amateur architect. Nicholas was the founder and benefactor of Rhode Island College, which later became Brown University. It was Joseph Brown who is credited with the design of the meetinghouse. In 1774 he went to Boston to appraise the prevailing trends in church architecture. He was evidently not impressed with what he saw because he turned to his copy of Gibbs' well-thumbed book. For the spire of the new church he selected the central engraving from Plate 30 (see photo page 129), where Gibbs had shown three alternate designs for St. Martin-in-the-Fields Church in London. Then Brown added, at its base, a modest Doric portico from the design for the Marybone Chapel. And in between, as evidence of the breadth of his derivations, if not his originality, he placed the now standard Palladian window surmounted by a pediment.

The whole design is not unattractive. It is a pleasant introduction to the eighty-foot square interior which again may be traced to Sir James Gibbs. The two-story Doric columns supporting the individual block entablatures and the rhythmic repetition of elliptical vaults in the plaster ceiling clearly recall the interior of St. Martin's Church.

A critical evaluation of the total design depends upon one's point of view. Pierson sums it up with his usual mixture of praise and condemnation. "It is one of the loveliest eighteenth century churches in America, yet with all its quiet dignity it is not a unified design. It is rather a series of 'quotations' performed in the neatest manner, and owes its delights not to Joseph Brown but to James Gibbs, the architect, and to the very special skills of James Sumner, master carpenter."

The official brochure by Professor Arthur Watson, on the other hand, states that, "James Sumner carried out the work of drawing plans to scale . . . and erecting the spire. To Gibbs must go full credit for the basic design; yet one must not forget that Joseph Brown chose and improved it with unerring taste." Needless to say, the graduates of Brown University, who have held their commencement exercises there since 1775, have their own subjective reactions. One might consider it in light of Churchill's oft-quoted and enigmatic dictum, "We shape our buildings and then they shape us."

You will, of course, make your own evaluation. But try, above all, to visualize this very special meetinghouse filled with that farsighted generation of early Americans who, through their faith, vision and industry created a monument that stands out far above its contemporary context of insincerity and absence of spiritual purpose. Providence's First Baptist Church is indeed a profound and permanent symbol which is obscured only by the magnificent trees that surround and dignify it.

The building was erected mainly by ships' carpenters who had been laid off when Parliament, following the famous Tea Party, closed the port of Boston. Under the direction of James Sumner, these men erected the 185-foot steeple by raising the telescoping sections, one after the other, "from the inside." The skill of the workmen bolstered by the church's strong spiritual foundations, must be largely responsible for the fact that the spire withstood the Great Gale of 1815 as well as the devastating hurricane of 1938.

The Brown family contributed generously to the total cost of 7000 pounds sterling for the completed structure and established an enviable tradition that has marked the history of Providence's First Baptist for two centuries. Their original gesture was echoed in 1958 when the resto-

First Baptist Church; Providence, Rhode Island

The most enduring quality of this interior lies not in its design but in its continued use and its associations

ration and rehabilitation were underwritten by a former graduate and Bible class instructor, John D. Rockefeller, Jr. of Brown University's graduating class of 1957.

Services: Sunday, 11 a.m.

Seating Capacity: 1400

Open to visitors: November to March, Monday to Friday, 10 a.m. to 2 p.m.; Sunday, 10 a.m. to 1 p.m. March to October, Monday to Friday, 10 a.m. to 3 p.m.; Saturday, 10 a.m. to 12 noon; Sunday, 10 a.m. to 1 p.m.

Telephone: (401) 751-2266

Construction Cost: Approximately 7000 pounds sterling.

How to get there: From Route I-95 East, take the first exit to downtown Providence. Continue past one traffic light, then turn left at Main Street. Proceed to 75 North Main at Waterman Street, near the bus terminal.

Architect: **Brown, Joseph,** merchant and gentleman-architect. 1733-1786. Born in Providence, Rhode Island. Brown studied the work of Wren and Gibbs. Work represented: First Baptist Church, Providence, Rhode Island. Brown also designed the first unit of Rhode Island University and several fine Georgian residences. He was later appointed Professor of Experimental Philosophy at Rhode Island College (later known as Brown University).

Alternate steeple designs for St. Martin-in-the-Fields

St Martin-in-the-Fields, London

The West Front

The portico of the Marybone Chapel, London

129

Portsmouth Priory Chapel; Portsmouth, Rhode Island

The hand of the craftsman;
the mind of the scholar;
the soul of the mystic.

Portsmouth Priory Chapel
Route 138, Portsmouth, Rhode Island 02871

Completed in 1960   **Pietro Belluschi, architect**

Tear yourself away, now, from the splendor of Newport's flamboyant secular buildings and the intriguing quality of its churches and head north, nine miles on Route 114, to Portsmouth.

Here, at Quaker Hill, there is a Friends meetinghouse, built in 1700 and still used for its original purpose. This was interrupted, incongruously, during the Revolution when this particularly peace-oriented structure was used as a barracks for Hessian troops. Except for the reverence due because of its age, it is less than distinguished architecturally.

Portsmouth's great contribution to the annals of the art of building is the Roman Catholic chapel in the Portsmouth Priory School. It was designed for the resident Benedictine monks in 1960 by Boston's Pietro Belluschi and is an early example of what is loosely termed "modern" ecclesiastical architecture.

The chapel is a minuscule masterpiece. It is one of the least self-conscious and least "dated" examples of the work of this half-century. One is introduced to its character by the variety and prominence of natural materials used on the exterior.

The building is impressive in its simple masses and is non-pretentious. But the interior, designed for worship and quiet meditation under the sure hand of a master, is a total success. It is undemanding and unaffected; it is particularly notable for the avoidance of obvious cleverness and originality.

This superb creation owes its supremely satisfying effect to the somewhat theatrical quality of the crucifix which consists of a tiny corpus seemingly suspended from radiating rays of light. It forms, naturally, the focal point of the whole composition and seems, at the same time, to embrace the whole of the interior. Richard Lippolt, well known for his huge suspended sculptures in Philharmonic Hall in Lincoln Center, has contributed this highly dramatic liturgical detail.

The interior as a whole has been unmatched until recently, when the chapels sheltered under the Citicorp Building in New York were brought to eloquent life by Louise Nevelson's breathtaking wood bas-reliefs.

The interior adheres to no particular style, yet it is organic in detail, faultlessly liturgical, and inspiring in the play of form and light as it seems to embrace and unite the entire congregation.

The Benedictine Order, noted in history for its famed Romanesque Abbey of Cluny in France, has contributed another place of prayer worthy of its long tradition of architectural excellence. It is another first for the Benedictine Order as well as for Rhode Island.

Services: Daily, 7:40 a.m.; Sunday, 9:30 a.m.; Vespers, daily, 5:30 p.m.
Open to visitors: The church is open daily.
Seating Capacity: 350
Telephone: (401) 683-2000
Construction Cost: Unknown.
How to get there: Portsmouth Abbey is located on Aquidneck Island, on Route 138, seven miles north of Newport, Rhode Island.

Architect: **Belluschi, Pietro** (see page 36).

Unitarian Universalist Society Church

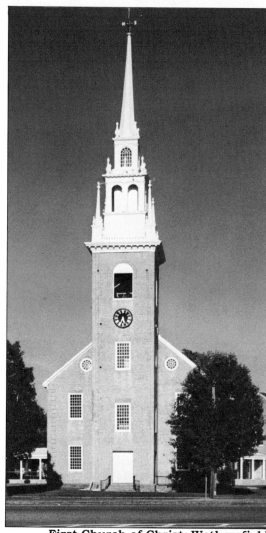

First Church of Christ, Wethersfield

First Church of Christ, Farmington

Old Trinity Episcopal Church

Connecticut's Oldest Churches

The four oldest existing churches in Connecticut are located in Wethersfield, Farmington, and Brooklyn, which boasts two of them. Brooklyn? Yes, Brooklyn! Not the one that bore that famous tree and those bums, the Dodgers, but a fully incorporated Connecticut town, with a population of five thousand, that contains more important religious edifices per capita than Rome itself.

Among the four there is an interesting correlation. Three, of course, are Congregational; the fourth is Episcopalian. Three are of the Wren-type, with the tower rising directly from the ground, and without the Gibbs-type portico. Three of them were erected in 1771, and all of them have been well preserved. And three of them are not "churches" at all, but meetinghouses.

The three Congregational houses of worship are distinguished by side entrances, with pews facing the pulpit at the center of the long side and not at the far end. This feature, though almost universally abandoned for over a century in favor of the regimented, "railroad-type" seating, has been revived, especially since Vatican II, throughout all denominations, because it automatically brings the congregation into intimate contact with the pulpit and the altar.

First Church of Christ; Wethersfield, Connecticut

First Church of Christ

250 Main Street, Wethersfield, Connecticut 06109

Completed in 1764   **John Chester, builder**

Wethersfield's First Church of Christ (the third on this site) was erected in 1764. It is one of the oldest brick churches in New England, where the local material was largely wood. (St. Luke's in Smithfield, Virginia, built in 1632, the oldest church in North America, is also in brick, the prestige material in that part of Georgian America.)

According to Fred Kelly, Wethersfield's church was long considered to be the finest church in New England outside of Boston. Its present exterior is indeed handsome, with an interesting pattern in brick, demonstrating a combination of dedication and skill. The side entrance leads to a much-renovated interior which retains little of its original quality. But the semi-circular seating clearly illustrates the psychological effectiveness of the lateral layout over the longitudinal plan due to the increased feeling of intimacy.

Wethersfield's Congregational Church adds its presence to the town's historical heritage. There are over one thousand buildings in the town's historic districts, all largely residential, that are considered worthy of the attention of the historian and the archaeologist.

Of minor but amusing interest is the fact that because the taxes required to finance the church were rather high, they were quite often paid not in coin of the realm, but with ropes of onions, the local product of the period.(The lowly onion, incidentally, along with radishes and garlic, is mentioned by Herodotus as part of the daily ration of workmen on Egypt's Great Pyramid.)

Services: Sunday, 9 and 10:30 a.m.   **Seating Capacity:** 500
Open to visitors: Monday to Friday, during business hours; Saturday by appointment; Sunday morning.
Telephone: (203) 529-1575
Construction Cost: Unknown.
How to get there: The church steeple is visible from Exit 26 off I-91. From the west, follow Connecticut Route 175 to Main Street. From the east, cross the Connecticut River to I-91.

Architect: Unknown. Builder's biography not available.

Now leave Wethersfield's pleasant timeless confines and brave Interstate 91 northward through Hartford, then take Interstate 84 going west for a trip of some twelve miles to Farmington.

If traffic permits, look back at the soaring spires of the nation's insurance centers. As they pierce the sky, they seem more to challenge each other than to defy gravity. Ask yourself if this phenomenon is not similar to the rivalry that inspired the lofty towers of the Middle Ages, and which, undeniably, contributed to the collapse of the 157-foot vaults of Beauvais Cathedral. Continuing the comparison, note that the Hartford Civic Center, the world's largest space-frame (a place of worship in its own right) also made history by crashing to the ground in 1977.

A few miles farther, the graceful geometric volumes of the University of Connecticut Medical Center, designed by Vincent Kling of Philadelphia, loom, majestic and disturbingly impersonal, to add another contemporary symbol to the horizon. The life of the spirit, economic security, and the assurance of the best of bodily care, all in a morning's panorama!

Now turn south on Route 10, and in a very short distance, one reenters the past.

First Church of Christ, Congregational

75 Main Street, Farmington, Connecticut 06032

Completed in 1771   **Captain Judah Woodruff, builder, designer**

Farmington's First Church rests, neither humble nor proud, but with dignity and complete self-assurance, on a knoll on the left. It is an image of worship in modest clapboard, but of far greater lineage and evoking a much deeper sense of inner satisfaction than its counterparts in concrete, steel and glass.

With its side entrance paralleling the street, and with the tower on the side rather than "in front," the building gives the impression of sliding down the hill. However, the First Church has stood for over two centuries, with the buildings of Miss Porter's School huddled about its base, and it promises to remain in place for a long time. There is not the slightest suggestion of collapse here, either imminent or remote.

This is again the third church building to occupy its site and is the work of a native son, Judah Woodruff. He had done his major work as a soldier and now turned his energies to building. Woodruff designed and supervised the erection of the church, but according to church records, he also had the dedication, the energy, the skill, and the time to design and carve the pulpit and the sounding-board overhead. His bill for the total project amounted to 1750 pounds, twelve shillings, ten and a half pence. This would amount to roughly $4000 at today's rate of exchange.

The guidebooks call attention to the fifty-two-foot-long twelve-inch by twelve-inch beams that were cut, trimmed, shaped and delivered and set in place, and from our mechanized frame of reference, we can only marvel at the effort and skill expended. But we do the Colonial workers an injustice. They are descendants of those craftsmen who, many centuries before, spanned the roof of the Great Council Hall in the Doge's Palace in Venice with the thirty-metre-long, thirty-inch-deep beams transported from Yugoslavia, without even leaving their initials. All in a day's or a week's work. They were simply maintaining an old tradition. Faith can move a forest as easily as it can move mountains.

There is an intriguing question of engineering in connection with the construction of the 150-foot spire on Farmington's First Church. In 1840 Noah Porter, then president of Yale University, stated that " . . . the spire was completed below and lifted to its place alongside the tower."

Trying to imagine the process of prefabricating, raising and moving the spire into position raises many questions. Was it actually built outside the tower and then raised? Would it not have been simpler to build the spire inside the tower and raise it vertically to its final position? This procedure has been mentioned as a possible procedure in the construction of New Haven's United Church (see page 177) a generation later. Ithiel Town, a competent engineer, must have known exactly what he was doing in New Haven. But considering the weight of the spire and the cross-bracing inside the tower, would it not have been still simpler and infinitely more logical to build both spires, piece by piece, *in situ?*

And one might ask, did not the same basic question arise in connection with every New England church? Perhaps we forget that spires have been built for centuries, even millennia, not in wood, but in heavy stone. Today, we tend to view the problem in terms of huge traveling cranes with 150-foot booms, and helicopters like the ones that were called in to set the spire of the new Coventry Cathedral (in England, not Connecticut) into its final position.

We forget that when we last climbed the towers of Notre Dame in Paris and admired those huge bronze bells, the guide told us that the thirteen-ton "Bourdon" was lifted into place, in 1750, in one and a half days. That makes the problem of the New England spire quite simple by comparison.

Services: Sunday, 10 a.m.
Seating Capacity: 600
Open to visitors: Monday to Friday, 9 a.m. to 4 p.m.
Telephone: (203) 677-2601
Construction Cost: Unknown.
How to get there: The church is located on Route 10, approximately one-quarter of a mile south of the junction of Routes 10 and 4 in Farmington Center.

Master-Builder: **Woodruff, Judah.** 1720-1799. Born in Farmington, Connecticut. He served as First Lieutenant in the French War and was at the battle of Ticonderoga. Woodruff built five houses in Farmington, all of which are still standing. He designed his masterpiece, the present Congregational church, at the age of forty.

First Church of Christ, Congregational; Farmington, Connecticut

Unitarian Universalist Society Church; Brooklyn, Connecticut

142

Unitarian Universalist Society Church
(Originally Congregational Church)
The Green, P.O. Box 38, Brooklyn, Connecticut 06234

Completed in 1772   **Architect unknown**

The plan of Farmington's church is similar to that of Wethersfield. Its spire is often compared to that of Old South Church in Boston. But in its entirety, Farmington Congregational Church has an almost identical twin in Brooklyn's Congregational Church at the extreme eastern border of the state.

With their solidly-based, Wren-style tower on one end, the two meetinghouses might have been built by the same man. But for Judah Woodruff (or anyone else), the straight-line distance separating them amounts to approximately fifty miles. On the other hand, if there were two designers, how could there have been collusion or even plagiarism since both churches were complete in 1771?

Only the dimensions differ. Farmington's audience room is fifty by seventy-five feet while Brooklyn's is forty-six by sixty feet. Both structures are in an almost perfect state of preservation. Like Wethersfield's church (and like most of France's great cathedrals) the names of the architect and builder have not been recorded.

Services: Second and fourth Sundays, September to December and April to June, 10:30 a.m.
Seating Capacity: 240 (will increase as restoration progresses)
Open to visitors: A key is available from the library across Route 149.
Telephone: None.
Construction Cost: Unknown.
How to get there: The church is on the Green, and is located at the intersection of U.S. Route 6 and Connecticut Route 169

Architect: Unknown.

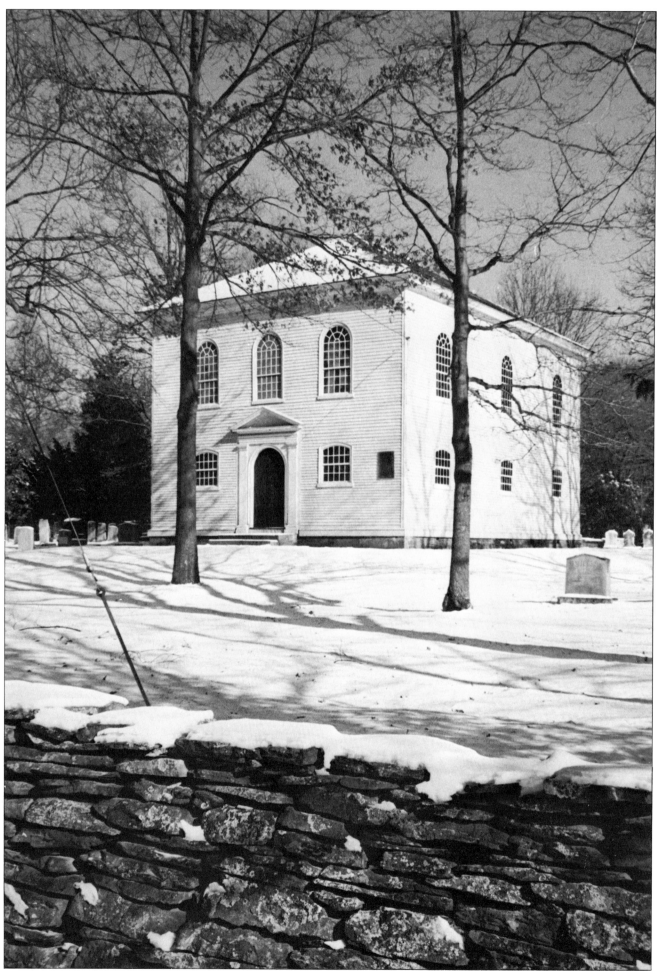

Old Trinity Episcopal Church; Brooklyn, Connecticut

Old Trinity Episcopal Church

Church Street, Brooklyn, Connecticut 06234

Completed in June 1770   **Godfrey Malbone, builder**

Brooklyn's Congregational Church belongs to the group of Georgian
churches that followed the Wren design accented by a spire. Brooklyn's
Episcopalian church, however, has a style completely its own, and a rich
background of legend as well. Without a spire, and with a rarely used
and most unecclesiastical hipped roof, "Old Trinity" looks more like a
meetinghouse than its Congregationalist contemporaries. But it is strictly a "church" because the Episcopalians did not apply the secular connotation to their houses of worship, least of all to this one. Its existence
is the outcome of interdenominational rivalry and is the result of the
presence of a single, most unusual and forceful individual.

Godfrey Malbone's name suggests a courtly, effete character in an
eighteenth century novel. His personality and temperament must have
been what we rather like to refer to as "typically American." He was
energetic, self-sufficient, aggressive, irascible, individualistic, and a most
resourceful example of the eighteenth century man. Not surprisingly,
Godfrey Malbone and his father enjoyed a comfortable share in
Newport's profitable rum trade.

He was understandably irate when he heard that his share of the
cost of a new Congregational Church (the one referred to above), to replace one that was only thirty years old, would be one-eighth of its total
cost. He expressed his indignation and his opinion of his colleagues
thus: "If those people had in mind to erect a square building this year,
then pull it down to erect a round one the next . . . must I share the
expense?"

He may have been unconsciously quoting Erasmus, who two centuries earlier in *The Praise of Folly*, referred to " . . . those men who suffer
from an incurable itch to be abuilding . . . they transform round structures into square ones, and presently square ones into round ones."

So Godfrey Malbone wrote, "I am but a poor architect . . . I have executed a small plan, 46' x 30', sufficient to answer our present purposes."
He went on, with the aid of his energy and charismatic personality, to
erect the Brooklyn First Episcopal Church, with a miniscule gallery,
coved ceiling (and a standard Episcopalian longitudinal plan) and com-

pleted it several months ahead of his Congregational rivals. And it was Godfrey Malbone himself who named it "Trinity Church."

Godfrey Malbone's father, incidentally, is buried in Trinity Episcopal Church in Newport, Rhode Island, below the area formerly occupied by his own pew (see page 121).

Services: Held only in August.
Seating Capacity: 125
Open to visitors: By appointment only; call the rectory.
Telephone: (203) 774-9352 or (203) 779-0138
Construction Cost: Unknown.
How to get there: Follow Route 6 north from Brooklyn for two miles to the flashing yellow light at Church Street. The church is one-quarter of a mile down Church Street.

Builder: **Malbone, Godfrey.** Biography not available.

A New England Mystery Play

History's horizon sparkles with architectural riddles. No one knows, for example, just how the pyramids in Egypt were erected. Or why the arches of Beauvais Cathedral collapsed. Or who built that extraordinary spiral staircase in the Loretto Chapel in Santa Fe, New Mexico.

One of architecture's unanswered questions is to be found in the heart of New England. Six of Connecticut's loveliest churches are eloquent, voiceless protagonists in a mystery which, like all the others, will probably never be solved.

Scene one takes place in the town of Milford, on the shore of Long Island Sound west of New Haven.

First Congregational Church, Southington

United Church of Christ, Milford

148

First Congregational Church, Cheshire

A New England Mystery Play

First Congregational Church, Old Lyme

First Congregational Church, Litchfield

First Congregational Church, Guilford

149

United Church of Christ; Milford, Connecticut

Scene One: Milford

United Church of Christ

34 West Main Street, Milford, Connecticut 06460

Completed in 1823   **David Hoadley, architect**

The First United Church of Christ (formerly First Church of Christ, Congregational) rises, graceful and proud, on the north edge of the town's business center. On windless days its spire and classic colonnade are reflected in the pool above the dam on the Milford River.

In its postcard setting, this prim yet imposing edifice connotes an era in civic and social serenity when the church was the major force in the community. Its presence is in startling contrast to today's world, whose myriad symbols seem continually in mutual contradiction.

The Milford structure is an excellent example of the Federal (or Late Georgian) style. It is basically a rectangular shell with a shallow gabled roof which traces its origin to the New England barn. It is heralded, however, by an imaginative spire that dates back to Sir Christopher Wren and his famous London churches, by the colonnaded entrance portico that recalls Palladio (and pagan Rome) via Sir James Gibbs, and by the fluted columns and Ionic capitals made famous by Venice's Vincent Scamozzi.

The interior is an architectural triumph. The central theme is the unity of the congregation and its concentration on the pulpit, the Protestant symbol of the Word. The desired effect is enhanced by the gallery on three sides.

The essentially Puritan character of the interior is alleviated by the elegant elliptical outline of the domed ceiling, accented by a huge brass chandelier. The studious avoidance of the use of color (an element considered unsuitable to the Puritan temperament) results in an effect that is almost theatrical. And when the sun pours in through two tiers of double-hung windows, the interior glows with an almost spiritual light.

The Milford church is a supreme architectural accomplishment. Its design, according to a bronze plaque half hidden in the grass, is attributed to "David Hoadley, Architect, 1823."

There is no sense of mystery here; only an inviting composition enclosing an inspiring space. One leaves with the flattering sensation of having been treated, gratuitously, to a work of art. One has learned to

expect this in the New England countryside; its recurrence, nevertheless, is a source of continuing pleasure.

Services: Sunday, 8:30 and 10:30 a.m.
Seating Capacity: 750
Open to visitors: Monday to Friday, 9 a.m. to 4:30 p.m.
Telephone: (203) 877-4277
Construction Cost: $7000
How to get there: The church is located behind the City Hall, and across the street from Milford High School.

Master-Builder: **Hoadley, David.** 1774-1838. Born in Waterbury, Connecticut. Hoadley's name is definitely associated with the design of churches in New Haven (see pages 179 and 181), Orange, Bethany, Norwalk, and Avon, all in Connecticut. Church designs attributed to him are: Milford, Cheshire (see page 155), Southington (see page 157), and Litchfield (see page 161), as well as Waterbury, Monroe, Huntington, and Hamden. Residences reputedly built from plans by Hoadley are to be found throughout Connecticut, notably in New Haven and Middletown. Hoadley died in obscurity. His body is buried in Waterbury, Connecticut.

The meetinghouse has broken out of its medieval shell and clothed itself in another, less rude, more sophisticated, less uncomfortable, but less intimate.

First Congregational Church; Cheshire, Connecticut

First Congregational Church
111 Church Drive, Cheshire Connecticut 06410

Completed in 1827   **David Hoadley, architect**

The ecclesiastical-architectural drama now leads us twenty miles north on Route 10 to the town of Cheshire (In the early 1800s the journey on horseback over dirt roads would have taken the better part of a day.).

Here, just as one had anticipated, the First Congregational Church, this time fronted by the spacious green, again lends special distinction to the town. How this vital element in urban planning, so frequently employed in times past and so rare today, contributes to an atmosphere of dignity and serenity!

Cheshire's church was dedicated in 1827, four years after Milford. Its colonnaded portico, subliminally suggesting confidence and stability, is similar to the one we have just seen. Its spire, consisting of seemingly disparate yet well-integrated geometric segments, seems likewise to lift the spirit heavenward. The ubiquitous weathervane adds an ironic note by reminding one of the vagaries of New England weather.

The interior, too, recalls the Milford church, with minor variations. Here the elliptical domed ceiling is reflected in the gentle curve of the pews; the center of the ceiling is accented by a circular ornament in carved wood from which the chandelier is suspended. In this case the chandelier is finished in pewter.

One is struck, as before, by the high quality of craftsmanship. The carved capitals, the rhythm of the modillions, the delicate moldings suggest a host of unknown, unsung artisans who, at this very moment seem to be sharing the atmosphere created by their works.

It is easy to minimize the obvious similarities between the two churches. Each one seems to possess its own individuality, and certainly neither edifice seems to suffer from the apparent cultural kinship.

Because of numerous details closely resembling corresponding ones in the Cheshire church, this church, too, is attributed to David Hoadley by historians Edmund Sinnott and Fred Kelly although, according to the latter, "A careful study of the society's records fails to disclose any reference to its designer."

Services: Sunday, 9 and 11 a.m.
Seating Capacity: 500
Open to visitors: Monday to Friday, 9 a.m. to 4:30 p.m.; Saturday, 9 a.m. to 12 noon.
Telephone: (203) 272-5323
Construction Cost: $6,872.59
How to get there: The church is located on Route 10, just south of the center of Cheshire.

Architect: **Hoadley, David** (see page 152).

First Congregational Church
37 Main Street, Southington, Connecticut 06489

Completed in 1830   **Levi Newell, Selah Lewis, builders**

Seven miles farther north on Route 10 the drama, which presumably is unfolding in our minds, takes an abrupt turn. Southington's First Congregational Church stands somewhat uncomfortably near the town's center. To view it to advantage one must cross Route 10 and reach the tiny patch of greenery that remains after a generation of soulless highway engineers have cruelly bisected the church's front lawn.

As one measures the church's proportions and assesses its detail, one is tempted to exclaim, "How typical!" But one is immediately struck with an overwhelming double sense of *deja vu*. On closely appraising the portico, the spire and the whole eminently satisfying facade, we realize that we have seen this church not once, but twice before. The fluted, half-reeded columns capped by those radiating volutes, the arched doorways, the modillions rippling along the cornice and up the rake of the pediment are similar, if not identical to what we have witnessed in Cheshire and Milford.

The square-based spire with its open arcaded belfry, the shuttered octagon and the slender cone terminating, predictably, in the wrought iron weathervane is an unmistakable echo of the church's two neighbors to the south.

The disturbing impression of repetition is reinforced in the interior, even after one has reveled once more in the symphony of space, form, and light. The curved banks of pews, the domed ceiling, the pewter chandelier, even the alternating sunburst-and-ginger-cookie ornaments of the gallery soffit follow a preestablished pattern. Only the pulpit itself is different.

Southington's church, in short, appears to be an outright replica of its predecessors. And here the element of mystery enters in. Was this church designed by one of Hoadley's contemporaries? It is conceivable that one of his rivals may have adapted Hoadley's design for Cheshire (completed in 1827 and a mere seven miles distant) in time for Levi Newell and Selah Lewis to begin construction in Southington in December, 1828. However, anyone capable of undertaking the design aspect of this project would surely have imprinted it with his own signature.

First Congregational Church; Southington, Connecticut

There are no substantiating records to resolve this nagging question. David Hoadley must have designed all three churches. But how could he have found the energy and the time, only five years after completing Milford and fresh from the year-old project in Cheshire, to add a third major challenge to his list? The question of logistics alone is staggering, to say the least.

***

Services: Sunday, 10 a.m.
Seating Capacity: 500
Open to visitors: Sunday to Friday, 9 a.m. to 12 noon.
Telephone: (203) 628-6958
Construction Cost: $6842
How to get there: The church is on Route 10, near the center of town.

Architect: **Unknown.**

First Congregational Church; Litchfield, Connecticut

First Congregational Church

Litchfield, Connecticut 06759

Completed in 1829   **Architect Unknown**

Litchfield in the early nineteenth century must have been a good two days' journey northwest from Southington. Even today there are no direct connecting roads. Here the mystery of Connecticut's four churches is fully compounded.

One has been forewarned. One is prepared for the possibility that the First Congregational Church may be a replica of its three predecessors. And at first glance, our fears are confirmed.

But what a replica! In its setting at the far end of a broad, wide esplanade, the effect of Litchfield's church is nothing short of spectacular. It does not dominate the green; it crowns it. Indeed, built on a slight rise, facing in a southerly direction, it seems to crown the entire state. And never was a queen more regal, more self-assured, and at the same time more gracious, more cordial, more generous with her presence!

Its white profile contrasts with its immediate entourage in all seasons. In this sense, Litchfield has given the New England Church a character as distinctive, in its own context, as that of Europe's great cathedrals.

The breathtaking ensemble of portico and spire which, together, seem to announce the sanctuary beyond, is almost identical to those of Southington, Cheshire, and Milford, but this factor does not detract in the least from the feeling of esthetic pleasure that Litchfield's church arouses.

Inside, the domed ceiling, the pews, the gallery, the columns are unmistakable duplicates of those we have seen just a few hours before. The pulpit, in fact, is identical to that in Cheshire. And the lighting, both by double-hung sash and by pewter chandelier, possesses the same luminous, almost theatrical quality.

But what makes Litchfield a special and unforgettable experience is its setting. Removed from the town's secular activity, yet not remote, its impact is further enhanced by strategically-located maple trees and the broad, restful expanse of the green itself. And the composition, from every angle, is blissfully devoid of overhead electric lines and telephone wires.

Before this supreme achievement in design and environment, the matter of similarities and prototypes becomes esthetically incidental and spiritually irrelevant. Litchfield's church is a thing of exquisite beauty in its own right. It was dedicated in 1829. The identity of its architect may never be known.

Services: Sunday, 10:45 a.m.; Communion, first Sunday, 7:30 a.m.
Seating Capacity: 350
Open to visitors: Daily, 9 a.m. to 5 p.m.
Telephone: (203) 567-8705
Construction Cost: Not recorded.
How to get there: The church is on East Street, facing the Green. The Green is at the junction of Routes 25, 63, and 118. Litchfield itself is in Litchfield County, about six miles southwest of Torrington on Route 202.

Architect: **Unknown.**

First Congregational Church
122 Broad Street, Guilford, Connecticut 06437

Completed in May 1830

Architect unknown
Builder unknown

The mystery of the almost simultaneous erection of these six fine New England churches is unsolved, and will probably remain so. For those who seek to oversimplify the explanation, let them add two baffling pieces to the puzzle.

Guilford's First Congregational Church joined the group of almost identical designs in 1829. The marked resemblance among the four meetinghouses with a fifth, in Guilford, is understandable. "Here the building committee was empowered, according to a notice in the *New Haven Register,* ". . . to contract with any suitable person or persons for the erection of a new house for public worship . . . to be finished nearly in the same style with the new churches in Milford and Cheshire."

The low bidders, Ira Atwater and Wilson Booth had only to refer to the established prototypes to fulfill their $6500 contract.

Services: Sunday, 9 and 10:30 a.m.
Seating Capacity: Approximately 400.
Open to visitors: Any time, by appointment.
Telephone: (203) 453-5249
Construction Cost: $7400
How to get there: Take exit 58 from I-95, and drive south toward the Guilford Green. The church faces the Green.

Architect: **Unknown.**

First Congregational Church; Guilford, Connecticut

First Congregational Church; Old Lyme, Connecticut

First Congregational Church

Ferry Road, Old Lyme, Connecticut 06371

Completed in 1817   **Original architect unknown**
Renovated in 1910   **Ernest Green, renovation architect**

Nothing has yet been revealed to explain the striking similarity among the five meetinghouses now listed, and a sixth in Old Lyme.

According to Edmund Sinnott, the present structure is an accurate and fireproof reproduction of the meetinghouse that burned to the ground in 1907. But Old Lyme's original meetinghouse, erected by Samuel Belcher, was completed in 1817, well before Hoadley (supposedly) designed the Milford church!

Is it conceivable that Hoadley took a page from Belcher's book, in the same way that Atwater and Booth derived their design from Hoadley's work? Or did Hoadley refer directly back to the same English sources as Belcher, who developed his design from plans brought from London by Colonel Charles Griswold? Or did Belcher himself actually design the four churches attributed to Hoadley?

No records of plans exist to shed any light on this matter. The network of unanswered questions is similar to the controversy over the true origin of Shakespeare's plays.

In the end, the identity of the designer, from an esthetic point of view is purely academic. The individual works of art do not suffer in the least, however, from their mutual resemblance. Indeed, far from detracting from their merit, their similarities seem to reinforce their claim to history's attention. They are examples of a style, not isolated accidents or personal expressions. As esthetic experiences, they are made individual by their location and their immediate environment. They are architectural gems, each one in its own right. Like identical pearls or rubies, they differ only in their setting.

Services: Sunday, 9:15 and 11 a.m.
Seating Capacity: 350
Open to visitors: Monday to Friday, 9 a.m. to 12 noon.
Telephone: (203) 434-8498
Construction Cost: Unknown.

How to get there: Going north on I-95, take exit 70, and turn right at the end of the ramp. Continue to the blinker, then turn left. The church is at the end of Ferry Street. Driving south on I-95, take Exit 70. Turn left at the end of the ramp, toward Long Island Sound.

Architect: **Unknown.**

A NEW ENGLAND MYSTERY PLAY

Similarities and Differences

The degree of similarity among the four churches is of undoubted interest, if only academically. Certainly the element of accident or coincidence must be ruled out.

The six floor plans are, of course, rectangular. The depth of the sanctuary varies from sixty eight feet in Cheshire to eighty four feet in Milford, but the width in all four cases is almost exactly fifty feet. Probably the pattern of the roof trusses (which are identical) was firmly fixed in a single designer's mind. Prefabrication, however, must be ruled out because of the obvious difficulties of transportation. Moreover, prefabrication from stock patterns would not have resulted in the variations that occur in the pitch of the four roofs.

The projection of the entrance portico varies from a minimum of five feet in Cheshire to eight feet in Southington, but the width in each case is twenty eight feet. The height of the columns, as well as the details of the fluting, reeding, and the surmounting Scamozzi capitals, is repeated without deviation. Here prefabrication is clearly indicated. It is known that one Hezekiah Augur carried on a thriving business of cabinet-making and ornamental woodwork in New Haven, and it is most likely that he made not only the sixteen portico columns, but the sixteen exterior pilasters and the interior colonnettes as well. This work, including the transportation of rough lumber from Vermont and the deliveries of the finished product, must have been a fairly profitable enterprise, even over a seven-year period. A similar situation existed in Rome, during the reign of the Emperor Hadrian. The sixteen granite columns and the marble capitals of the Pantheon were prefabricated and shipped from a thriving studio in Alexandria. In both cases, it is difficult to imagine the existence of a serious competitor.

All six spires are square at the base, developing into two diminishing octagons to support the slender conical top. The surface filigree shows some individuality in design. But the six weathervanes, as far as can be ascertained by binocular observation, might have been cast from the same mold.

The entrance doors are identical in width and in height. Only the pattern of the paneling differs. All twelve doors are topped with semi-circular transoms with identical wood carved keystones. And the leaded fan lights differ only in one case.

Windows throughout are twenty-over-twenty double-hung wood sash. Individuality in fenestration occurs only in Cheshire, where an impertinent window mars the tympanum, and in Milford, where a window is inexplicably crowded into the base of the spire.

The ceiling domes are identical, reflecting the design of the scissor-trussed roof. The central ornament, which is absent only in Milford, is identical in design though not in diameter. The interior capitals are replicas in miniature of those on the exterior, and finally, the soffits throughout are adorned with alternating sunburst-and-ginger-cookie decorations. They must, without question, have originated in the same atelier.

For this accumulation of parallels, similarities, and coincidences, all appearing with the briefest of history's moments, there can be no simple explanation!

Finale

The mystery of the six almost identical Connecticut churches leaves a fascinating trail of unanswered questions. How could one man, working over a sixty-mile stretch, design, supervise and construct six major projects within the space of five years and leave no clear record of his achievements?

Since no "plans" as such have been discovered, it is certain that a minimum of time was spent at the drawing board, and that many design decisions were made either by means of simple notes or verbally, on the site. If so, were these directives transmitted to trained and trusted construction superintendents, as is the custom today? This would contradict the prevailing notion that Hoadley was the typical architect-builder, like the *maitre d'oeuvre* of the middle ages, who directed the entire work from the "lodge" adjacent to the site.

And assuming the best of conditions, even admitting the likelihood that major elements such as columns, windows, doors and moldings were prefabricated from standard designs, the realities of the construction process present a stream of difficulties. How could one man travel from one site to another, battling the problems of weather, communications and deliveries, and the complications of logistics that plague builders even today?

The design and construction of a simple wooden church, using the full range of computers, bulldozers, and power tools to replace the ox, the windlass, the axe and the adze could take eighteen months today and still be subject to weather conditions. The creation of the four churches leads one to imagine that, short of divine intervention, some special ingredient existed of which we have no knowledge. If Hoadley had maintained a central office similar to that of Charles Bulfinch in Boston, he might have delegated various aspects of the projects to trained subordinates. But as far as is known, Hoadley never had an established practice to match Bulfinch's sophisticated organization. Boston in the 1820s was far more advanced in every respect than rural communities of Connecticut.

Little is known of Hoadley's private life or his approach to the art of building. There is even some controversy as to whether he actually merited the title of architect, although Fred Kelly, dean of chroniclers of Connecticut meetinghouses, insists stoutly that Hoadly was a full-fledged architect as well as a builder in the full sense of both terms. He is known to have been born in Waterbury in 1774. There is incontrovertible evidence that he contributed to the design of eight churches and it is generally assumed that he took part in at least six others.

Beyond that, it is recorded only that he died in obscurity in Waterbury in 1838, penniless, like his colleague Thomas Jefferson. But at least Jefferson enjoyed the honor of public recognition during his own lifetime.

The Double Triad
New Haven and Hartford

During the eleventh century, according to the French medieval chronicler Raoul Glaber, it seemed as though "the very world wished to clothe herself in a white mantle of churches."

The same colorful phrase might be applied, with apologies, to nineteenth century New England. In Connecticut alone some seventy churches, erected between 1800 and 1830 are still in existence; of these, thirteen were completed during 1827 and 1828. And to reinforce the metaphor, most of these were sheathed in wood clapboard painted white. The churches described in the chapter entitled "A New England Mystery Play" are typical of the period.

The New Haven Triad

The New Haven Triad of churches offers a fascinating series of exceptions to the standard exteriors. Two edifices in red brick and one in brown granite grace the spacious green. In a town richly endowed with buildings of special interest, they are the city's prime historic landmarks.

The three churches are in excellent condition and have been in continuous use since their completion in 1814 through 1918. They seem to enjoy a life of their own, apart from that of the town and the university, both of which, despite their strong religious heritage, seem to be more and more engulfed in temporal preoccupations. Without the three churches, the vast green, although lined with the city's famed elm trees, would be no more than a dull if verdant oasis, an interruption in the city's daily activity. But with the triad, the green becomes the frame for a living record of New Haven's spiritual, economic, and architectural history.

Their positioning is striking. Their arcades are in a mutually respectful straight line, as though each one is careful not to claim undue prominence. All face the east, as if to proclaim a similar purpose. And to add to the atmosphere of tolerance, they are separated by less than a hundred-yard dash of lawn, a feature which at the same time connects them.

Two are designed in the Federal style, with a red brick "sanctuary" and white spire, and house the Congregational faith. The southernmost is Neo-Gothic in style, in brown granite ashlar, and its community is Episcopalian. All three were completed between 1813 and 1815.

The United (or North) Church was built by David Hoadley from a design by Ebenezer Johnson. It is without doubt the finest work of this prolific architect-builder whose name is associated with at least sixteen churches in southern Connecticut (see page 152).

The other two, one Federal-style and Congregational, the other Neo-Gothic and Episcopalian, are attributed, in greater part, to Ithiel Town, a noted architect-engineer and inventor of the lattice truss. Like many of his colleagues today, Town had a special way with words. He wrote of the New Haven Triad, "The situation of the three churches, in line and nearly equidistant, and viewed in connection with other buildings in the square, is not surpassed by any arrangement in this country."

Ithiel Town's generalization is difficult to challenge. Nowhere, either here or abroad, not even in the city of London (where Christopher Wren was able to squeeze some fifty churches within a one-mile square) does a similar "situation" exist.

But "nowhere," indeed! As usual, for every rule there is at least one exception, and this time a grand one. By a coincidence worthy of the status of phenomenon, an almost identical "situation" exists in the center of Hartford, thirty-nine miles to the north on Route 91.

The Hartford Triad

The capitol's Main Street is generously lined with important historic structures, recalling the *Avenue des Monuments* in Ghent, Belgium. The Old State House, designed by Boston's Bulfinch, the Neo-Gothic Athenaeum by Henry Austin, and the Neo-Classic Library, not to mention the grandiose headquarters of the city's huge insurance companies, are but a few of the masterpieces that distinguish the city.

But nestling comfortably between these are three religious buildings of great architectural interest. They are the South Church, the Center Church and Christ Church Cathedral. This is the Hartford Triad.

The three churches are separated by a few blocks of commercial structures. Considered together, however, they are an almost exact mirror-image of their counterparts in New Haven. All are in a straight line, and all of them face the east. And unbelievably, two are in the Federal style in a red brick and white trim, and house the Congregational persuasion; the third, this time the northernmost, is Neo-Gothic, in brown sandstone, and is the seat of the Episcopalian Bishop.

The dates of completion bracket those of the New Haven Triad. The Center Church was dedicated in 1807; the South Church and the Cathedral both in 1827. The latter, which at first glance, closely resembles Trinity Church in New Haven, is attributed, with only a minor element of uncertainty, to Ithiel Town.

The Double Triad

The six churches, whether considered as two sets of three or as individual creations, are of special interest for an accumulation of reasons. Each one has been a vital and thriving factor in the life of its community since its dedication. Each one reflects the differences, and the similarities, of the beliefs that inspired them and maintain them. Each represents a step in the progression of historic "styles" that is characteristic of the architecture of the entire nineteenth century.

None was designed by an "architect" as we know him today. One at least was the work of the architect-builder, an age-old profession (now sadly extinct) of which David Hoadley was an outstanding practitioner. Three of them, on the other hand, show the handprint of the amateur-architect, Ithiel Town, who was drawn to the art of building through his cultural background but who did not depend on it for his livelihood. Ithiel Town belonged to this latter group of nineteenth century Renaissance men, as did the statesman-architect Thomas Jefferson, and William Thornton, a doctor of medicine who made the first design for the National Capitol.

The two triads, furthermore, are products of the phase in the development of the art when a designer might, with equal facility (and without the slightest esthetic compunction), design in two totally foreign styles. Town's two immediately adjacent projects, the extremes of Federal and Gothic, were produced almost simultaneously. It is worth noting, in this context, that Benjamin Latrobe in 1804 submitted a Gothic design for the Baltimore Cathedral, along with the Neo-Classic Pantheon-influenced design that was accepted and built. A near-century later, Cass Gilbert, with no recorded twinge of his creative conscience, designed the neo-Classic Supreme Court Building in Washington, D.C., the pseudo-Gothic Woolworth Building and the Beaux Arts-Renaissance-Revival Customs House in New York City within the span of a decade.

The variety of architectural experiences in the two triads dramatizes the denominational need for architectural individuality. In the design of Christ Church in Hartford, the Reverend Nathaniel S. Wheaton was influenced by his enthusiasm for the towering lancet-style spires of York Minster, which he had recently visited. It seemed only natural to him to adopt an image differing from that already used by the prevailing Congregationalists, by whom the Episcopalians were greatly outnumbered. Thus the English Gothic symbolizes the emergence of a new faith in an area already well populated by descendants of a group that, two centuries before, had "dissented" against those very same Anglicans. It is no surprise that early in the twentieth century, the National Episcopalian Shrine in Washington, D.C., proudly began displaying its now well-established English Gothic lineage.

This multi-faceted aspect of religion's and the nation's history is revealing as well as highly reassuring. The various denominations, with their deeply ingrained differences, were founded and still flourish in an atmosphere of healthy cohabitation. Their architectural images are tangible evidence not only of the validity of their beliefs, but of the rich soil of tolerance that granted them their first building permits. They are substantial evidence that the translation from less receptive soil was justified, and that the Bill of Rights is consistently adhered to. The motto of the state of Connecticut, *"Qui Transtulit Sustinet,"* freely translates as, "He who brought us here will sustain us," is also not intended to be exclusive in any sense.

This freedom of expression is a typically American phenomenon. In almost every other country, a single architectural style proclaims the identity of a major denominational presence. In the United States, some 240-odd varieties of religion line the streets of our cities, villages and towns.

One wonders, particularly in consideration of the apparent futile efforts to "unite" the churches, if it was not intended to be that way after all? Is it not possible that the Architect of the Universe prefers the prevailing varieties and imagination in form, color, texture and ritual? Is it not possible He is pleased, even flattered, by the rich variety and limitless imagination in the form, color and texture of "His House"?

The New Haven Triad

United Church-on-the-Green

Trinity Episcopal Church

Center Church-on-the-Green

174

The Hartford Triad

First Church of Christ

Christ Church Cathedral, Episcopal

South Congregational Church

United Church-on-the-Green; New Haven, Connecticut

United Church-on-the-Green

323 Temple Street, New Haven, Connecticut 06511

Completed on November 29, 1815

**Ebenezr Johnson,
David Hoadley, architects**

Services: Sunday, 11 a.m.
Seating Capacity: 800
Open to visitors: By appointment; call the Parish House.
How to get there: The church is on the New Haven Green, near Elm Street.

Telephone: (203) 787-4195 or (203) 787-4196
Construction Cost: Not recorded.

Architects: **Hoadley, David** (see page 152).
        Johnson, Ebenezr. Biography not available.

Puritan restraint still prevails, but pagan details and classic elegance begin to appear.

Center Church-on-the-Green; New Haven, Connecticut

Center Church-on-the-Green

311 Temple Street, New Haven, Connecticut 06511

Completed on December 27, 1814

Asher Benjamin, architect
Ithiel Town, builder, designer

Services: Sunday, 10:30 a.m.; 10 a.m. in summer.
Seating Capacity: Approximately 800.
Open to visitors: Tuesday to Friday, 10 a.m. to 12 noon, 1 to 3 p.m.
Telephone: (203) 787-0121
Construction Cost: $35,000
How to get there: The church is on the New Haven Green, directly in front of the Yale University campus, and is the center one of the three churches.

Engineer and Architect: **Town, Ithiel.** 1784-1894. Born in Thompson, Connecticut. Town was a carpenter who became a gentleman of leisure through the invention of the Town Lattice Truss. He studied with Asher Benjamin and was later associated with Isaac Damon in the construction of Center Church in New Haven. At the same time Town designed Trinity Church in New Haven and later Christ Church Cathedral in Hartford. As a partner in the firm of Town and Davis in New York, Town designed the Yale College Library, the Wadsworth Athaneum in Hartford, New York City's Custom House and the State Capitols of Indiana and Illinois. Ithiel Town's remains are buried in New Haven's Grove Street Cemetery.

Trinity Episcopal Church; New Haven, Connecticut

Trinity Episcopal Church

956 Chapel Street, New Haven, Connecticut 06510

Completed in 1814   **Ithiel Town, architect**

Services: Sunday, 8, 9:15, and 11 a.m.; Wednesday, 12 noon; Tuesday, 5:30 p.m.
Seating Capacity: 1000
Open to visitors: Monday to Friday, 9:30 a.m. to 5 p.m.
Telephone: (203) 624-3101
Construction Cost: $29,000
How to get there: The church is on the Green, at the corner of Temple and Chapel Streets.

Architect: **Town, Ithiel** (see page 179).

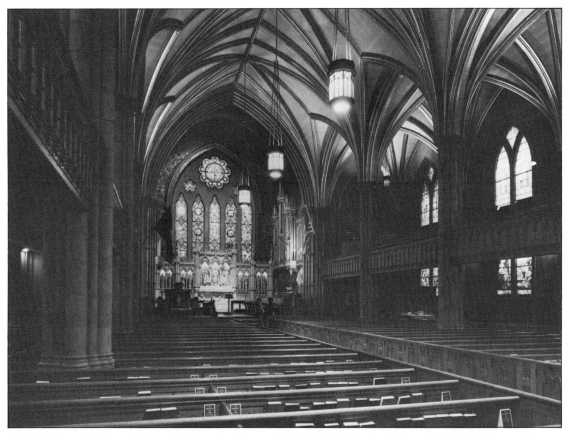

The Goths, after overthrowing pagan Rome, invaded Protestant New England.

First Church of Christ; Hartford, Connecticut

First Church of Christ

60 Gold Street, Hartford, Connecticut 06103

Completed in December 1807   **Daniel Wadsworth, architect**

Services: Sunday, 11 a.m.   **Telephone:** (203) 249-5631
Seating Capacity: 800   **Construction Cost:** $32,014.26
Open to visitors: Daily, 12 noon to 3 p.m.
How to get there: From I-91, take the Capitol exit to Main Street. The church is at the corner of Main and Gold Streets, opposite the Travelers' Insurance Building.

Architect: **Wadsworth, Daniel.** Biography not available.

The Reformation resides in a setting of Roman grandeur.

South Congregational Church; Hartford, Connecticut

South Congregational Church

277 Main Street, Hartford, Connecticut, 06106

Completed on April 1, 1827

**Colonel William Hayden, architect
Captain Nathaniel Woodhouse,
builder, designer**

Services: Sunday, 10 a.m.; Thursday, October to May, 7:15 p.m.
Seating Capacity: Approximately 1000
Open to visitors: Monday to Friday, 9 a.m. to 4 p.m.
Telephone: (203) 249-8627
Construction Cost: $23,000
How to get there: The church is at the corner of Main and Buckingham Streets. It is easily accessible from the Capitol Avenue exit off I-84, and the Capitol Avenue exit from I-91.

Architect: **Hayden, William.** Biography not available.

The exterior is Federal, but the interior is Baroque, and is splendid.

Christ Church Cathedral, Episcopal; Hartford, Connecticut

Christ Church Cathedral, Episcopal
45 Church Street (office), Hartford, Connecticut 06103

Completed in December 1827   **Ithiel Town, architect**

Services: Sunday, 8 and 10:30 a.m., 4:30 p.m.; Monday to Saturday, 12 noon.
Seating Capacity: 900 to 1000.
Open to visitors: Daily, 8 a.m. to 5 p.m.; Saturday, 8 a.m. to 4 p.m.
Telephone: (203) 527-7231
Construction Cost: $43,706.19
How to get there: The cathedral is at the corner of Main and Church Streets. It is near the Trumbull Street exit from I-84 East, and Exit 32 off I-84 West.

Architect: **Town, Ithiel** (see page 179).

The church strikes an early Neo-Gothic tour de force.

A Gothic Pilgrimage

"Gothic" means a pointed arch. "Gothic" means a Charles Addams cartoon. "Gothic" means cathedrals, castles, mystery, intrigue, trapdoors and dungeons.

But "Gothic" also designates man's highest achievement in the use of stone in building. The physics of native materials, the demands of the church and of society, and the challenge of esthetics combined to create the great cathedrals of the thirteenth century, eighty of which were erected in France alone. With the simplest of hand tools, with no machines more sophisticated than the windlass and a source of power limited to the lowly ox, the *maitres d'oeuvres* combined the pointed arch, the flying buttress, and the ribbed vault from which the resulting style derived its original name "Ogival."

The later appellation "Gothic" was applied, at first, in a highly pejorative sense. Its origin is attributed to the Renaissance architect-artist-writer Giorgio Vasari. He and his sixteenth-century colleagues, inspired by new discoveries, explorations, translations, and above all a vast new world of wealth and ambition, set out to revive the culture of ancient Greece and Rome. And in order to downgrade the art that had symbolized the culture of the three preceding centuries, Vasari used the name of the barbarians who had contributed substantially to the destruction of the Roman Empire, the Goths.

Classical art and architecture thus became the source of all artistic inspiration through the Renaissance, the Mannerist and the Baroque periods, until it climaxed in a fascinating, operatic burst of Rococo art in the mid-eighteenth century.

Then, suddenly and inexplicably, the term "Gothic" underwent the phenomenon of melioration. Writers, poets and architects revived Gothic architecture in particular with the same enthusiasm and freedom that the Renaissance men had revived the classics. And countryside and city-side, especially in England and in the newly formed United States, were enriched by man's capacity for fantasy, irrationality, romance, and above all, his inherent nostalgia.

It is particularly interesting in this context, that in 1804 the noted

English-born American architect, Benjamin Latrobe, proposed the Gothic style for Baltimore's new Roman Catholic Cathedral in order to symbolize "the medieval Catholic heritage." Shortly thereafter, however, he obligingly submitted an alternative design derived from the Pantheon in Rome and justified it because it represented "patriotic Americanism" as well as "loyalty to Rome." Obviously the influence of Thomas Jefferson was still quite strong, and Gothic architecture was not quite ready for its inevitable rebirth.

But New England was in a sense, more forward-looking. Ithiel Town, native of Connecticut, designed the Center Church in New Haven (aided by Isaac Damon) in 1814. Then in 1817, responding to the Episcopal tendency to distinguish itself from other denominations, he designed and built Trinity Church, a bare hundred yards to the south. To add to this revealing mélange, in 1827 he made a proposal for the Connecticut State Capitol in Greek Doric, to be situated almost between the two preceding structures. The state capitol was never built: we are not convinced that it was either a blessing or a pity.

But how fortunate, nevertheless, that so many examples of the facility of the human hand, the mind, and the imagination still remain to enrich our cities! We have only to visit them and explore them in this light to appreciate (at literally no expense) the wealth and variety of our experiences in religious architecture alone.

The following pages list two examples of the wide range of expression within a single style that remain to illuminate our past and brighten the present.

Dwight Chapel; New Haven, Connecticut

Dwight Chapel

67 High Street, New Haven, Connecticut 06520

Completed in 1842   **Henry Austin, architect**

Dwight Chapel, in a grassy courtyard off High Street, is a place of worship. It adds an accent of reverence to one of the university's gracious quadrangles, and in appearance, it could not be more appropriate.

But it has a curious history. Yale's first neo-Gothic building was designed in 1841 as a library! Henry Austin, facile architect of the neo-Egyptian entrance to the Oak Grove Cemetery, adapted the design of "Old Library" from a drawing for St. Katherine's Hospital in London. It was after a pious suggestion by the architect John Russell Pope that it was transformed, with a minimum of change, by Charles Klauder of Philadelphia.

The same John Russell Pope designed the Payne Whitney Gymnasium which, even to the least sophisticated eye, looks very much like a church. This may well be because its huge central tower is an almost exact duplicate of the central element of Liverpool's Anglican Cathedral. The latter, to further compound the confusion of tongues, was designed, not in the Middle Ages, but by Sir Giles Scott in 1903.

One wonders if William of Sens, the French *maitre d'oeuvre* who brought Gothic architecture to England from France in the twelfth century, is still resting quietly in his grave?

Services: Multi-denominational services are held throughout the year.
Seating Capacity: 300
Open to visitors: Daily, 9 a.m. to 5 p.m.
Telephone: (203) 436-1480
Construction Cost: Not available.
How to get there: Go west along Chapel Street for one block beyond the Green, then turn right. Dwight Chapel is a half-block down, on the right.

Architect: **Austin, Henry, AIA.** 1804-1891 Born at Mt. Carmel, Connecticut. Austin was a carpenter's apprentice who later studied architecture in the firm of Town & Davis. Work represented: Old Yale Library (now Dwight Chapel). Other important works: New Haven Savings Bank, City Library and Grave Street Cemetery. He also designed Moses Yale Beach House in Wallingford, Connecticut and the Morse-Libbey House in Portland, Maine.

Saint Mary's Roman Catholic Church; Stamford, Connecticut

A GOTHIC PILGRIMAGE

Saint Mary's Roman Catholic Church
566 Elm Street, Stamford, Connecticut 06902

Completed in June 1928   **O'Connell & Shaw, Inc., architect**

The unmistakable silhouette of this striking church rises serenely, almost disdainfully above its low-rise surroundings, recalling the typical French (and Canadian) church-dominated villages. It was designed in 1928 by Frank O'Connell, architect of Boston, and erected by the firm of Diekenborn of Waterbury, Connecticut.

St. Mary's Church is characteristic of the second wave of neo-Gothic structures, and as one might surmise from the dedication date, the grand finale of the Revival Period. It is eclectic in the highest degree and is most impressive, despite the deterioration of its milieu, and the fact that, in addition, it lacks the broad park-like surroundings of its English antecedents.

The interior, though rather dark, is awesome in its mystic grandeur. It breathes all the haunting atmosphere that seems to have made Gothic the most inspiring and most conducive to reverence of all the styles in history's rich storehouse.

St. Mary's Church in Stamford is an invitation to ponder once again the intriguing question of the psychological effect of structure. Does one stand in respectful awe of the Gothic because its slender, uninterrupted colonnettes carry the eye and the imagination and the spirit upward, without interruption, and holds them there effortlessly suspended, at the juncture of its delicate arches?

Certainly the effect is different from the one produced by the semi-circular arch, which carries the same human attributes upward but returns them without interruption and somewhat disappointingly down to their earthbound point of departure.

Is it not generally agreed that the Gothic structural system, with its inherent spaciousness and lightness, suggests freedom and release, whereas the Roman and the Romanesque impose a sensation of power and authority and absolutism?

One cannot deny that if the expression, in stone, of freedom of thought did not actually pave the way for the Reformation, it must have provided an admirable and most provocative stage-setting. And one is reminded that the counter-Reformation, with its return to formality and discipline, was clearly illustrated in history's pages by a return to the dominating and discipling effect of the dome and the official abandonment of the soaring symbol of the tower and the spire.

It is an avenue of debate best left to those who attempt to interpret architecture in terms of human psychology, but it deserves to be seriously considered. St. Mary's is an indisputable case history of what may happen to a beautiful structure when no civic nor religious body exists to preserve it from the ravages of time; when the inexorable march of what is loosely termed progress abandons an entire section of a city to deterioration and worst of all, when the cruel process of parish gerrymandering leaves a splendid structure without commensurate means of support.

Today, we are condemned (in fulfillment of Santayana's dictum) to repeat the past, but not because we cannot remember it. We seem to have gone out of our way, in many cases, to ignore it.

———

Services: Sunday, 7, 8:15, 9:15, and 10:30 a.m., and 12; Monday to Friday, 7 and 9 a.m.; Saturday, 7 and 9 a.m., 12:15 and 5:15 p.m.
Seating Capacity: 900
Open to visitors: Open daily 8 a.m. to 7 p.m.
Telephone: (203) 324-7321
Construction Cost: $519,000
How to get there: Take the Elm Street exit from the Connecticut Turnpike; go south on Elm Street to the third light.

Architect: **O'Connell, Frank.** Biography not available.

Saint Nicholas Russian Orthodox Church
37 Lake Street (rectory), Stratford, Connecticut 06497

Completed in 1942   **A. E. Boldakoff, architect**

When the first Russian immigrants arrived in America, they brought with them a tradition of ecclesiastical architecture that has remained almost intact for over fifteen centuries.

Unlike the Puritans (or Separatists, or Congregationalists, if you will), who invented the square wood-framed meetinghouse to suit their special requirements, the Russians retained the architectural ambience that has characterized the Orthodox church since the twelfth century and which, structurally, still reflects the Byzantine breakthrough of the sixth century A.D.

Traveling along Route 91 east of Bridgeport and looking north, one is startled by the sight of eight flame-tipped towers rising above the New England foliage. Except for the absence of the usual birch trees, one might easily imagine oneself on the outskirts of Moscow or Kiev, where numerous examples of Russian Orthodox architecture have been preserved as museum pieces.

St. Nicholas Russian Orthodox Greek Catholic Church (its full designation) was erected in 1942 by a small group of Russian employees of the Sikorsky Aero Engineering Corporation who migrated to Stratford when the plant itself was moved from its original location in College Point, Long Island. Igor Sikorsky, who perfected the first commercially practical helicopter, was, understandably, on the building committee and one of the principal donors to the project.

Today the huge Sikorsky plant, a division of United Technologies, dominates the northern boundary of Stratford; the likewise internationally-famed American Shakespeare Theatre accents its southern shore. And the minuscule St. Nicholas Russian Church rises in between to complete the unique religious-cultural-industrial triad that distinguishes this diminutive Connecticut town.

The architect of the church was A. E. Boldakoff, with R. N. Verhovsky, laureate of the Russian Academy of Art, as consultant. The dedication ceremony was attended by the Metropolitan Theophilus, head of the Russian Orthodox Church in all of the United States and Canada. (Two years later the Metropolitan returned to honor the church at a special

Saint Nicholas Russian Orthodox Church; Stratford, Connecticut

Mass in commemoration of the 150th anniversary of the founding of the Russian Church in this country.)

The exterior is a joyous composition in form, line and the arabesques of its detail. It is as distinctively Slavic as the music that accompanies the services. The exterior scale is deceptive; the full capacity is a surprising 400 persons.

The exterior and the interior both provide an object lesson in the "Novgorod" style. The central dome is supported by the pendentives that first made architectural history in Santa Sophia in Constantinople in 537 A.D. The focal point of the interior, the Iconostasis, or "Image-Screen," was designed by the architect-builder Boldakoff.

There are dozens of Orthodox churches in New England; there are five in Bridgeport alone. But among them all, St. Nicholas in Stratford, for its charm, its individuality, and special quality of serendipity is an architectural historian's treasure.

Services: Sunday, 10 a.m.; Saturday, 7 p.m.
Seating Capacity: 400
Open to visitors: By appointment; during services.
Telephone: (203) 375-2786
Construction Cost: Not available.
How to get there: Get off I-95 at the Lake Avenue exit. You will see the spires of Saint Nicholas to the north, two blocks away. The church is opposite a supermarket.

Architect: **Boldakoff, A. E.** Biography not available.

The inside of a diamond

First Presbyterian Church

1101 Bedford Street, Stamford, Connecticut 06905

Completed in 1958   **Wallace Harrison, architect**

In 1956 A.D. a gigantic crystal sprang out of the ground in the area known as Stamford, in the province of Connecticut. Or so it might appear to a visitor from outer space who, at first glance, would probably classify the First Presbyterian Church as another of geology's inexplicable phenomena.

And in a sense, he would be right. In its form and texture, this unique edifice resembles nothing so much as one of those fascinating natural formations that one discovers from time to time in the infinite realm of the physical world.

The church is indeed a thing of the earth. It is built, not "upon a rock," but of an ingenious amalgam of baked limestone, sand, gravel and water veined with iron, a blend of silicon, potassium and lead, and a final sheathing of rough slate. Its sophisticated geometry could hardly have been conceived by man who, with rare exceptions, limits himself to variations of the cube, the sphere and the tetrahedon.

Its exterior is but a meager clue to the structure's full significance. Wallace Harrison, its architect, has created a work of infinite dimensions which the visitors, whether extraterrestrial or earthbound, can only appreciate from the inside.

Unlike their Protestant colleagues, who, in a tradition of self-imposed abstinence, have eschewed the use of color, the Presbyterians in this case have embraced it in all its pre-Reformation splendor.

The translucent walls, criss-crossed by the silhouette of structural ribs, create a chromatic fantasy that sparkles with every change of sky and sunlight. Blended imperceptibly with the roof, they appear to envelop the congregation in a multi-colored cloak. The effect is as theatrical as it is protective. It is, as one parishioner remarked, "like being on the inside of a diamond." The effect is matched only by the greatest of the medieval cathedrals. It is no coincidence that the use of modern inch-thick "faceted" or "chipped" glass originated in the town of Chartres itself.

Stamford's "Fish Church" (sometimes referred to affectionately as "The House of Cod"), is a very special house of worship. It arouses the

First Presbyterian Church; Stamford, Connecticut

full range of both objective and subjective reactions.

The structural engineer will be intrigued by the triangular precast panels which, not unlike a house made of mutally-balanced playing cards, are interconnected to form a huge polyhedron. It is a masterpiece of design and execution. But the structure's engineer may be totally unaware that the essential bonding ingredient is provided by the presence of the Holy Spirit.

In its intrinsic symmetry the Harrison church (unlike Rowayton's dynamic swirl) represents a universe of simple, basic truths with no extraneous challenges. For all the drama provided by the interior light, the slightly splayed ranks of pews and the gently inward-sloping walls focus the attention directly on the silhouette of the Book, the denominational insignia.

Stamford's First Presbyterian Church is the visual embodiment of

St. Paul's definition of faith, "The substance of things hoped for, the evidence of things not seen." Its commanding physical presence is filled to overflowing with the abstract connotations of that special quality that is fundamental to all of religion. Seldom have the architect, the pastor and the builder worked together in greater unison.

Shortly after the appearance of the sanctuary, there occurred another phenomenon. A slender, 260-foot organism composed of bone and sinew, closely resembling a tower in reinforced concrete, rose out of the ground nearby. It is used today to support a fifty-six bell carillon so that the passing populace, absorbed in temporal preoccupations, may be reminded by sound as well as by sight of the presence of the church itself. The tower has contributed immeasurably to the church's popular appeal, and is an essential part of its image.

Although the church seats 800 persons, the masterful handling of scale and detail have given it a special feeling of intimacy. The entire sanctuary could, in fact, be fitted inside the nave of St. Joseph's Cathedral in Hartford (see page 215). But the Glory of God, to whom all churches are dedicated, is not measured in feet, meters or even cubits. St. Joseph's Cathedral itself, including its spire, could be set inside the nave of St. Peter's Basilica in Rome with room to spare.

Services: Sunday, 10:30 a.m.

Seating Capacity: 700

Open to visitors: Daily, 9 a.m. to 4 p.m.

Telephone: (203) 324-9502

Construction Cost: Approximately $850,000.

How to get there: Take the High Ridge Road exit from the Merritt Parkway, or the Elm Street exit from I-95, and ask for further directions. The church is just northeast of the business center of Stamford.

Architect: **Harrison, Wallace Kirkman.** FAIA. Born in Worcester, Massachusetts in 1895. Harrison was educated at Worcester Technical Institute. He held a principal position in the firm of Harrison and Abramovitz, New York for many years. Work represented: First Presbytrian Church, Stamford, Connecticut.Other important works: Rockefeller Center, United Nations Building, New York, Lincoln Center, New York, Albany Mall, Albany, New York. He received the Gold Medal American Institute of Architects, 1977. (Wallace Harrison is not related to the eighteenth century gentleman-architect, Peter Harrison.)

The church's interior, an extraordinary concept, is a realization brilliant in many ways.

Notre Dame Motherhouse Chapel; Wilton, Connecticut

"Give us a beautiful chapel!"

Notre Dame Motherhouse Chapel
Belden Hill Road, Wilton, Connecticut 06897

Completed in 1960   **J. Gerald Phelan, architect**

Until the spring of 1958, 345 Belden Hill Road was a forty-two acre plateau covered with second-growth, sloping gently down to the west, with nothing to distinguish it except for a fieldstone residence of no special lineage. Today it is the site of "Wilton Motherhouse." It is the center of the Northeastern Province of the School Sisters of Notre Dame, a religious order founded in Germany in the early nineteenth century.

The two and one-half story, slate-roofed structure in honey-colored brick also houses an educational institution where, until 1970, young girls passed through the stages of postulant, novice, junior and senior before taking their final vows as teaching nuns.

Though it appears to be little more than a large rambling residential structure, the Motherhouse contains all the facilities for a fully-accredited college. There are bedrooms and dining accommodations for some 280 sisters. There are offices, classrooms, laboratories and a large library. There is an assembly room affectionately known as the "Atrium" and there is also a full-size gymnasium. And, of course, a chapel.

The separate facilities radiate from a five-sided court accented by a bell-tower, recalling the typical medieval cloister. The pentagonal court was selected over the square, the hexagon and the circle because it accommodated the broad physical requirements of the institution. This seldom-used plan adds a note of distinction, associating the building (although somewhat incongruously), with the Pentagon in Washington, and also with the Renaissance Palazzo Farnese in Caprarola, Italy.
The high point of the composition is the chapel. This dominant feature is the culmination of a historic interview among the Provincial, Mother Paschal, her two associates, Sister Emmanuel and Sister Theodora, and her architect.

Mother Paschal did not present the architect with the usual detailed program of requirements. Nor, to the architect's utter astonishment, did she mention a budget. She simply made it clear that it was the architect's function to provide everything, in proper order and scale, to meet the requirements of the combined residence and college; the details were to be ascertained through observation and consultation with her associates. But she listed her personal desires in a single sentence: "Don't give us any flat roofs; don't give us any wet floors, and please, give us a beautiful chapel!"

The architect's response to the three-pronged challenge is a matter of history. It is a monument to faith and trust – and evidence that the "dream" client has not yet ceased to exist.

The Notre Dame Motherhouse is dominated by the chapel that proclaims the building's identity and purpose. As if to introduce an element of suspense, the chapel is approached through a long, low corridor that connects it to the main building. At its far end, two oak doors open to reveal a space whose essence can only be described as one of total serenity. The atmosphere of quiet drama achieved through its architecture is not immediately perceived; it is felt. It is – to borrow a phrase from Le Corbusier – "a place of silence, of prayer, of peace, of spiritural joy." This is the heart of the order. And as the Sisters enter and exit silently for worship, for communion and for meditation, the space seems to pulsate with the life that it shares with them.

Its structural skeleton, visible inside as well as out, does not lead the eye dogmatically upward in the traditional sense, to be lost in a maze of self-conscious and distracting engineering. Instead, the profiles of the monolithic concrete buttresses are sloped inward, and as they diminish in size and in span, they lead the eye gently toward the altar. The crucifix, a corpus of laurel wood suspended on a rough cross of hand-adzed silver-weathered chestnut, is silhouetted against a pattern of tilted polished stone surfaces that crown it with a nimbus of ever-changing reflections.

The construction of the chapel is "modern," but the effect is frankly traditional. A visiting artist, responding to the universal impulse to make comparisons, exclaimed, "It is a cathedral!"

It is doubtful whether a consciously "contemporary" solution would have produced the same effect. The integration of the buttresses with the ceiling beams, outlined with soft indirect lighting, is reminiscent of the great churches of the Middle Ages. But it is the lightness in construction revealing the maximum of outside light that creates the full effect. There are no supporting walls. The spaces between the buttresses are filled, from floor to ceiling, with stained glass. The fourteen panels are the work of Vytautas Jonynas, a native of Lithuania, who was awarded the commission as a the result of an international competition. The seven north panels depict incidents in the life of the Blessed Mother; those on the south, the life of Christ. The setting sun reflects these scenes onto the south faces of the buttresses in summer and on the north in winter, and the effect is nothing short of breathtaking.

When a chorus of young sopranos and altos fills the nearly perfect acoustical shell with Gregorian chant, even the most unbelieving must be aware that no mere mortal, working alone, could have achieved this effect. The integration of construction and finish, flawlessly executed to conceal its intricacy, is largely the inspired work of Danny Pica, one of

The nimbus that appears over the Crucifix was not in the architect's plans.

the gifted construction superintendents for the E&F Construction Company.

But there is far more here than careful design and studied execution. No one visiting the chapel doubts that it was the pure and powerful faith of Mother Paschal that made it initially possible. And only the most rigid iconoclast will deny that the Holy Spirit must have directed the hand of His earthbound surrogate in the rare and special privilege of drawing the plans.

Services: Private

Seating Capacity: 500

Open to visitors: Daily; apply to the portress at the main entrance.

Telephone: (203) 762-3318

Construction Cost: $3,300,000

How to get there: Take Exit 40 from the Merritt Parkway, then Route 7 north for four miles. Turn left at Wolfpit Road. Drive two miles to Belden Hill Road, and turn left. Motherhouse is 200 yards beyond on the right.

Architect: **Phelan, Gerald, FAIA.** Born in Bridgeport, Connecticut in 1893. Phelan was educated at Pratt Institute in New York. He was president of the firm of Fletcher-Thompson, Inc. Architects & Engineers from 1942 to 1972. Works represented: Ascension Church, Hamden, Connecticut and the SSND Motherhouse, Wilton, Connecticut (see pages 203 and 219). Other important works: Fairfield University, Notre Dame Catholic High School and St. Vincent's Hospital, Bridgeport, Connecticut, Shadowbrook Novitiate in Lenox, Massachusetts. He was made a Fellow of the American Institute of Architects in 1968 and received an Honorary Doctorate from Fairfield University in 1972.

Saint Mark's Episcopal Church; New Canaan, Connecticut

Saint Mark's Episcopal Church

111 Oenoke Ridge, New Canaan, Connecticut 06840

Completed in 1962   **Sherwood, Mills & Smith, architect**

Follow Main Street northward for a quarter-mile past two white clapboard "Colonial" churches where it becomes Oenoke Avenue, and one is rewarded with an architectural composition that is reserved, austere and yet quietly striking.

St. Mark's Church faces south over a broad expanse of lawn dotted with aged elms and maples, a setting to rival the most gracious of the English cathedrals. It is a studied juxtaposition of aspiring verticals in the tower and in the church balanced by the broad horizontal profile of the offices and classrooms. There is a quiet, harmonious contrast between the grey-brown rough brick walls and the smooth white concrete skeleton.

But the interior, though conventional in plan, is marked by an ecstatic outburst of unbounded creative enthusiasm. The structural reinforced concrete frame, in the Gothic tradition, has eliminated the supporting wall. The entire east wall has thus been lighted and lightened by the use of faceted glass, the material that was used without reservation in Stamford's First Presbyterian Church and in St. Joseph's Roman Catholic Cathedral in Hartford.

In St. Mark's, however, the architect, with admirable restraint, has limited the articulation of this important area to a geometric pattern of small glass panels. The reason, perhaps not immediately apparent, has been to avoid an embarrassment of riches, an artistic confusion that might result because of the dominating effect of the full-height bronze reredos which climaxes the interior.

This imaginative concept and masterful realization is an open grillwork of light vertical bars overlaid by two dynamic swirls complementing each other in a manner similar to the reverse curves seen in Oriental symbolism. Throughout this basic design are placed some 150 metal sculptures representing Biblical symbols and illustrations related to man's redemption. The reredos was designed and executed by the sculptor, Clark B. Fitz-Gerald.

The effect of the whole, matched by the perfection of execution, recalls the powerful overall impact followed by the detailed treatment revealed at close range that one experiences in the windows of a thirteenth century cathedral. It is a monumental work of art. St. Mark's Church in New Canaan makes the work of Coventry Cathedral in England (also completed in 1962) seem labored and self-conscious by comparison. St. Mark's Church is a significant architectural experience at still another level. It was designed by Willis N. Mills, FAIA, father of Willis N. Mills, Jr., designer of the Episcopalian-Presbyterian ensemble in Wilton (see page 235). It is interesting to note how the span of a mere generation, in different forms and vocabulary, but with the same aim, the same sincerity and equal creativity, may result in a fascinating variation of the same timeless statement.

Services: Sunday, 8, 9:15, and 11 a.m.
Seating Capacity: 750
Open to visitors: Monday to Friday, 8:30 a.m. to 4:30 p.m.; tour guides on notice.
Telephone: (203) 966-4515
Construction Cost: Unknown.
How to get there: The church is one-half mile north of the center of town, on Route 124.

Architect: **Mills, Willis N., FAIA.** Born in Menominee, Michigan in 1907. He was educated at the University of Pennsylvania and was a former principal partner in the firm of Sherwood, Mills and Smith in Stamford, Connecticut. Work represented: St. Mark's Episcopal Church, New Canaan. Other important works: Science Building Kent School, Dormitory Berkeley Divinity School, New Haven in Connecticut and IBM Buildings in Poughkeepsie and Endicott, New York and in Rochester, Minnesota. Mills was made a Fellow of the American Institute of Architects in 1963.

Creation, redemption, and infinity are caught in an inspired instant.

United Church; Rowayton, Connecticut

United Church

210 Rowayton Avenue, Rowayton, Connecticut 06853

Completed in 1962   **Joseph Salerno, architect**

The first reaction of many who view the odd-shaped edifice on Route 136 for the first time is, "It doesn't look like a church!" And they are right. The United Church of Rowayton bears no resemblance whatever to the prim white-spired meetinghouse one might expect to find in this typical New England community. For this reason it has been the source of a continuous outpouring of colorful comparisons.

Some visitors have compared it to a Mexican hat. Others, recalling St. Augustine's phrase, "The church is a ship," have likened it to a billowing sail.

A neighbor, actress Mildred Dunnock (quoting both St. Matthew and St. Luke), said it looked very much like a mother hen setting over a brood of chicks. And those who said that it approximated the shell of a conch are mindful of the fact that Le Corbusier, in designing the roof of his famed Chapel at Ronchamp, was inspired by the shell of a crab.

The list of metaphors evoked by this provocative structure is endless. But it is most significant that this highly original concept, in its totality, is a deliberate metaphorical representation of the nature and aims of the congregation that made it possible.

The building committee, headed by its far-seeing pastor, Donald W. Emig, outlined their needs simply. "We want a house of worship that will fulfill the needs of this community, not one in San Fancisco or Albuquerque. We are unique."

The last three words of their charge must have sounded like celestial music to the ears of their architect, Joseph Salerno of Westport. Soft spoken, erudite, philosophically-inclined, he outlined his concept of the church building thus. "It is a table, a cross, and a pulpit surrounded by people." In a single phrase, he summed up the intrinsic unity, the ecumenical dimensions, and the spiritual aspirations that were later embodied in his design. Aided by the breadth of vision of the committee, and bolstered by his own creative convictions, he was able ultimately to achieve one of the New England region's most ingenious solutions in church architecture.

Every aspect of the completed structure seems eminently appropri-

The interior of Noah's Ark might have looked like this, except that the Ark supposedly had only one window.

ate to its use. The semi-circular seating pattern, with everyone "within smiling distance from each other," is a bold step away from the standard arrangement in parallel rows. The free form enclosing the 300-member congregation is an eloquent envelope that ascends ninety feet above the floor in an effortless arabesque, culminating in a shaft of light. In the union of wall and roof, Salerno has added a touch of genius. He has gone a step beyond Frank Lloyd Wright, who referred to the spire of one of his churches as "a finger pointing toward God." Salerno has made the entire church into an upward-aspiring symbol.

The wood used throughout is so natural, so appropriate and so expertly handled that one is unaware of the high degree of engineering required to achieve the church's unique contours. The individually shaped laminated ribs and the planking in compound curves reflect the origin of the material. How foreign cold, hard concrete or intransigent welded steel would have been! And what other surface than a shaggy shingled exterior would echo so well the character of the surrounding residences?

The Rowayton Church is a superbly functional unit. Though it is several light years removed from the rigid geometry usually associated with the term "functional," it serves the varied needs of the parish to perfection.

And it is "organic" in the full definition of the word. As it embraces the knoll, inviting the outside world into its folds, the United Church seems to rest in the modest self-assurance that, in this context, no other design would have been possible. One can easily imagine Louis Sullivan and Frank Lloyd Wright at this moment, in some Elysian drawing-room, beaming in benign approval.

From the day of dedication the United Church has been an unbounded functional and esthetic success. In 1963, in the prestigious company of Eero Saarinen, Minoru Yamasaki and representatives of Skidmore, Ownings, and Merrill, Joseph Salerno was awarded the top annual honor by the American Institute of Architects.

But he was more recently accorded the ultimate accolade. In exceptional cases the profession grants to the designer a permanent moral equity in his creation, so that we now speak of Saarinen's TWA Terminal, Frank Lloyd Wright's Falling Water, as well as the Eiffel Tower. Today, the United Church of Rowayton is often referred to as "Salerno's Church."

The tribute is well deserved. The vision of its designer, the wisdom of its pastor and the judgment of the building committee have combined to create a living expression of a living, working faith. And in what better way could one honor "the Architect of the Universe"?

Services: Sunday, 10:15 a.m.; Summer, 9:15 a.m.
Seating Capacity: Approximately 285.
Open to visitors: Daily, 9:30 a.m. to 4 p.m.
Telephone (203) 866-1415
Construction Cost: $351,000 (including pipe organ)
How to get there: The church is located on Route 136, near the Darien town line. It is not far from the Rowayton town center.

Architect, **Salerno, Joseph, AIA.** Born in Chicago, Illinois in 1914. Salerno was educated at Yale University. Work represented: United Church, Rowayton, Connecticut.* Other important works: Synagogue, Harrison, New York, Educational Buildings in Westport, Middletown, Scotland, Norwalk and Weston, Connecticut, residences in Weston, Redding, Westport, Connecticut and Rye, New York, Hotels in Canada, Thailand, Venezuela, Italy, Hawaii and the British West Indies.

*This project received the First Honor Award from the American Institute of Architects in 1962.

Cathedral of Saint Joseph; Hartford, Connecticut

Cathedral of Saint Joseph

140 Farmington Avenue, Hartford,Connecticut 06105

Completed on May 15, 1962   **Eggers & Higgins, Inc., architect**

Early in the twelfth century A.D., in the rebuilding of the Abbey of St. Denis, Abbot Suger and his *maitres-d'oeuvres* were "impelled to reject the forms of the past and to strike out in entirely new directions." the result was the first completed Gothic edifice. The Ogival style (later termed "Gothic" by the Renaissance writer Vasari) was "a new concept of architectural space and light," and the art of building advanced a giant step. (The quotations are from Whitney Stoddard's *Monastery and Cathedral in France.)*

In 1957, after the Cathedral of Hartford had been destroyed by fire, Archbishop Henry J. O'Brien instructed his architect to design "a church contemporary with the times in which it is to be built." Today, the new Cathedral of St. Joseph rises imperiously on Farmington Avenue, at the edge of the city's business district. It is a significant departure from the tradition that dates back eight centuries. Though not a herald of "modern" design, it is an important voice in the chorus that responded to the architectural implications in Pope John's plea to "let a little light into the church."

The new edifice, dedicated in 1962, is a simple, solid mass relieved by strong verticals. It is surmounted by a towering 256-foot carillon-tower whose splayed profile seems to add to its height. The building is neither traditional nor derivative in any sense. There are no flying buttresses, no pointed (or round) arches, no finials or crockets to acknowledge the accepted vernacular. However, the sculptured stone panels over the entrances are the aesthetic equivalent of the medieval tympanum, and the carved bronze doors reflect, in miniature, the entrances to St. Peter's Basilica in Rome. The rounded apse which develops as a continuation of the nave is similar to that of the mighty fortress-cathedral of Albi in southern France.

The interior is a triumph of variety in unity. Here, too, there is none of the spatial restlessness of the Gothic style which, though it has made the church a sanctuary for centuries of esthetes and romanticists, sometimes detracts from the atmosphere of worship and meditation. The absence of transepts, triforium galleries and side aisles goes unnoticed.

The four-foot wide side aisles, fully accessible yet unobtrusive, are skillfully hidden on the periphery of the nave.

The most striking feature of the interior is the 18,000 square feet of brilliant "faceted" glass that seems to sparkle with every change, either in the outside light or in the position of the viewer. This contemporary feature, which is responsible for the visual impact of the abstract patterns in the Stamford Presbyterian Church (see page 198), here represents scenes from the Scripture in broad realistic strokes.

The solidity of the almost three-dimensional effect is especially appropriate to the reassuring sensation of strength and security that the concrete structure itself evokes. The fragile one-eighth inch glass, set into lead *cames* in the medieval manner (which is used with great effectiveness in the Motherhouse Chapel in Wilton (see page 203) would have been totally ineffective in the context of the Cathedral of Hartford's Roman Catholic Diocese.

The ceiling which from time immemorial has been articulated with structural tracery, is given over to a galaxy of brushed-aluminum stars which dispense a benison of indirect lighting and air-conditioning.

The reinforced concrete skeleton is not specifically expressed, either inside or out. Nevertheless, St. Joseph's Cathedral is truly contemporary with its time. Through a careful avoidance of the passing clichés (not the least of which is Louis Sullivan's dictum "Form follows Function"), it has achieved a measure of timelessness worthy of an archdiocese. One wonders what would have appeared on this superb site if the architect had been seduced by Felix Candela's flowing concrete shells, or the brilliantly conceived concrete honeycombs of Pier Luigi Nervi? Or the uncompromising individuality of Le Corbusier, whose revolutionary Chapel at Longchamps had only recently burst upon the horizon?

There is a philosophical challenge implicit in the juxtaposition of the cathedral with the Georgian-style seat of the Aetna Insurance Company immediately opposite. Though St. Joseph's Cathedral, frankly speaking, suffers somewhat from the absence of the grand *parvis* that is climaxed by Notre Dame in Paris, or the vast, paved squares that precede the cathedrals of Milan and Cologne, it seems to share the broad grassy esplanade that separates and connects it with its commerce-oriented neighbor. Together both buildings share a verdant ambiance in a form of symbiosis that is as historically revealing as it is environmentally enriching.

The list of participants in this creation reads like the peerage of the building industry. The prestigious firm of Eggers & Higgins was the architect; the firm of Syska & Hennessey was the mechanical consultant, and the George A. Fuller Company the general contractor. The dependence on foreign sources for its special accoutrements is apparent throughout. The faceted glass is from France; the carved stone and bronze and the monumental ceramic mosaic reredos are by the Institute of Liturgical Art in Rome; the marble throughout is from Italy. The

The space, dignity, and grandeur are worthy of a great cathedral.

twelve bronze bells, though designed in Cincinnati, Ohio, were cast in Holland.

The limestone sheathing of the exterior is from Alabama, the interior veneer from Indiana, and the granite base is from New Hampshire. The 3400 pews on two separate and almost equal levels are of American walnut. The aluminum used in the forty-foot-high baldachino covering the altar can almost certainly be traced to the bauxite mines of Arkansas; the 8000-pipe organ was fabricated in Hartford.

A broad span of earthly space is represented in Archbishop O'Brien's "contemporary" cathedral. Its spirit, however, far transcends the times in which it was built.

Services: Sunday, 7, 8, 9:15, and 11 a.m., 12:15 and 5 p.m.; Daily Masses, 6:45 and 7:30 a.m., 12:10 p.m.; Saturday Vigil Mass, 5 p.m.
Seating Capacity: 1750
Open to visitors: Sunday to Saturday, 9 a.m. to 5 p.m.
Telephone: (203) 249-8431
Construction Cost: Not available.
How to get there: From I-84 East, take the Sisson Avenue exit. Turn right at the first light. Go on to the next light, and turn right onto Farmington Avenue.

Architect: **The Eggers Group, Inc., P.C.,** Architects and Planners, New York, New York. Work represented: St. Joseph's Roman Catholic Cathedral, Hartford, Connecticut. Other important works: Numerous religious, education and athletic facilities at Fairfield University, Columbia, Pace, Rutgers, as well as Nassau Community College, New York and the New Jersey College of Medicine and Dentistry.

Ascension Roman Catholic Church; Hamden, Connecticut

"Build me the finest church in all New England!"

Ascension Roman Catholic Church
1050 Dunbar Hill Road, Hamden, Connecticut 06514

Completed in September 1968   **J. Gerald Phelan, architect**

If Father John Cotter had lived in the thirteenth century France, he would undoubtedly have set out to erect a church to rival Notre Dame de Beauvais, with its 157-foot high vaulting. His assignment to Hamden, Connecticut in 1966 provided a somewhat different ambience in time and space, but it did nothing to diminish his desire. His first instruction to his architect was an unequivocal directive to surpass anything that had already been done. The only significant standards by which Father Cotter's success can be measured are his own, to be sure. But there can be no doubt that when, during the dedication mass, the sun shone through the skylight over the sanctuary and enveloped the head of Christ, no priest, regardless of his century, could have asked for more.

And while this meteorological and ceremonial coincidence is repeated annually (depending upon the whims of New England weather), Ascension Church and Hall is a remarkable structure for a multitude of other reasons.

Its dramatic profile crowns the highest point in the northern suburbs of Hamden. The broad low element to the right, as one approaches it, is the parish hall, housing the secular activities from weekday dinners, suppers and lectures to dances, bingo and basketball. The ascending feature on the left is the space reserved for worship. The two are connected by a common vestibule. The union of the two aspects of the church is a clear metaphor of the expanded line of the contemporary Roman Catholic community since the historic *Vatican II*. The hall is horizontal, earthbound, static; the church is vertical, soaring, dynamic. And yet they are not two structures, but two inseparable and integral parts of a single organism.

Structurally, Ascension Church and Hall is an exciting exercise in the flexibility of precast concrete and the lightness and daring of post-tensioning, the method by which the reinforcing steel is subjected to maximum stress after the concrete has set. Under the guidance of German-born structural engineer Heinz Jensen, the design is climaxed by a shaft eighty feet high, eight feet wide, and an incredible eight inches in thickness. The design is surmounted by a stylized image of the risen

219

The fifteenth Station of the Cross is molded in sculpture and in light.

Christ, a feature that further enhances the lightness of the whole composition. This effect is the result of the perfect balance between tension in the reinforcing steel (imported from Japan) and 5000 pound (per square inch) concrete in compression.

Though the whole may, from certain points, be dwarfed by the 529-foot spire of the Cathedral of Ulm in South Germany, Ascension is a logical candidate for the world's record in a monolithic spire.

The interior of the parish hall is no more nor less than one would expect in a structurally utilitarian multi-purpose space. But the interior of the church itself is a revelation. The entire concept, both as a whole and in detail, is a series of stimulating surprises. The floor plan is a spiral with the altar as its center. The wall surfaces are in rough concrete in flat planes separated by full height areas in abstract patterns of stained-glass. The rough-sawn oak seating concentrates on the altar in an intimate, sloping near-semicircle. The altar and the baptismal font both have polished top surfaces, but the sides are articulated by the drill-holes that, from time immemorial, have been used to release granite blocks from their natural beds.

The true glory of Ascension Church is the series of plaster bas-reliefs that adorn the left side wall and the sanctuary. They depict the Stations of the Cross in a continuous portrayal, culminating in the sanctuary area. Here, the fifteenth station, in acknowledgement of the church's name, is represented in a magnificent reredos crowning the main altar. These fascinating sculptures are the work of Donald Shepherd, an inspired artist who created these masterpieces of modern religious art in fresh plaster *in situ*. The instantaneous demand for concept and execution always at the mercy of an impersonal and impatient medium, represents the same demand for skill and motivation that resulted in the frescoes in Rome's Sistine Chapel.

A supremely satisfying sense of unity pervades this unusual structure. It is designed at the human scale, and furthermore, the hand of the craftsman is in evidence throughout. It is a triumph of coordination among architect, artist and builder, and the Client Himself (represented, of course, in the person of the pastor). It has achieved the immortality that far transcends the short span of all those who assisted at its creation.

Services: Sunday, 9 and 11 a.m.; Saturday, 5 and 6:30 p.m.
Seating Capacity: 550
Open to visitors: Daily, 10 a.m. to 5 p.m.
Telephone: (203) 288-7649
Construction Cost: $996,000
How to get there: From Exit 60 on the Wilbur Cross Parkway, take Dixwell Avenue south to Benham Street. Turn right and continue to Dunbar Hill Road for one mile. The church is at the top of the hill, on the left.

Architect: **Phelan, J. Gerald** (see page 205).

First Unitarian Church, Westport – 1964
The First Unitarian Congregational Society, Hartford

The number of ways that man has devised, and may yet conceive, to contain his need to worship cannot be counted. And one might well say, with all proper respect, thank God for that.

It has been estmated that some five million edifices have been erected in the service of Christianity, and that some three and a half million are still in existence. The varieties of religious experience, expressed in architecture, are infinite. But we have attempted, all too often, to confine these within a system of so-called "styles" which have acted as a series of prisons in which man's creativity has been confined, sometimes for centuries, rather than expanded and developed.

In the last half-century, however, man and his architect have been miraculously released from this bondage. Dating from the world financial crisis of 1929 through 1931, and the felicitous advent of the Bauhaus, this factor has pervaded all of western architecture. And it is particularly apparent in the design of churches. Two Connecticut churches by the architect Victor Lundy are paradigms of this timely phenomenon.

One is in Westport, the other in the outskirts of Hartford. Both respond to the relatively free requirements of the Unitarian persuasion. But they are radically different in form, in plan, even in the basic materials used. And they reflect no known style or idiom. They are unusually dissimilar: they echo only the vocabulary and the individual inflections of the architect himself.

The First Unitarian Church in Westport is essentially a system of curved wooden ribs starting, almost level, at the entrance and ascending in a sweep of compound curves to a fifty-six-foot climax over the chancel. Except for the fact that the ribs are convex rather than concave, they recall the hull of a ship. This time St. Augustine's "ship" appears in the form of a pagan Viking vessel, striding proudly, and not in the least incongruously, over the brow of a densely wooded hillside.

Hartford's First Unitarian Congregational Society Church, on the other hand, is situated in a large open park. It is circular in plan; structural supports for the roof consist of an octet of concrete vanes, radiating from the center of the design. The resulting very real spire arises proudly in the viewer's imagination. And as the Westport church recalls the symbolic bark so often associated with scripture, the interior of the Hartford church, with its sweep of curved wooden strips places the congregation within the center of a huge and equally symbolic fountain.

The two churches have been eulogized at length in professional and liturgical journals. Surprisingly, not the least revealing are those verbal appraisals offered by the architect himself.

But after the churches and their accompanying descriptions have been objectively evaluated, one is struck by a singular fact. The lyrical, imaginative and often scholarly encomiums that these two unusual creations inspire are not needed to enhance, or even document their effect. More often than not, they do less than justice to their subject. The buildings themselves seem to soar, well above the sea of accompanying aphorisms.

The phrase "soaring timbers," used to introduce the Westport church is not only rather clumsy; it is basically incorrect. The structure is not made of "timbers" in any sense. It is made of highly sophisticated carefully shaped laminated and glued wooden arches whose resulting lightness makes the roof seem to float over its slender metal supports in a manner that timbers could never match. Out of fairness, however, the reference to Hingham's Old Ship Meetinghouse is not inappropriate. In addition to being at once an accredited architectural and Unitarian shrine, the roof of the Old Ship is indeed made of real oak timbers, some of them, surprisingly, shaped to a rude curve. But they have not, to date, acquired the ability to soar.

Furthermore, the terms, "timeless, not transient form" may have been applied by the local chroniclers to the current church at any time in history. And the carefully contrived skylight, formed to "allow the universe to come in," is not restricted to the "duality of Unitarianism": it is precisely the light that Abbott Suger asked from his *maitres d'oeuvres* in the twelfth century and it was echoed by Pope John XXIII in our own time when he exhorted his flock to "let a little light into the church."

In short, all the facile and highly quotable verbal images demonstrate the utter futility of attempting to enclose a truly great creation within the framework of mere words. Those who view these two highly original structures will be made aware, once more, of a basic fact: that architecture at any level is its own script. If this were not so, there would be no need for the "art" of building, as we know and enjoy it.

True inspiration needs no accompanying libretto. Conversely, mediocrity in design does not deserve one. A poor design cannot be elevated beyond its own built-in limitations. And a great work of architecture speaks for itself.

The ultimate limits of religious expression are the bounds of man's creativity. And for this recurrent revelation we have God again to thank. He did not change man's tongues at Babel in order to confuse them, but to introduce them to the infinite range of human expression. At Beauvais, likewise, he caused the arches (the "soaring stones") to collapse as a tacit but emphatic sign that, for all the engineering and mystic marvels of Gothic architecture, he was impatient with the continual striving for height and bigness for their own sake.

In our own time, in order to encourage man to seek out new atmospheres of worship, He caused him to abandon the death grip of the Beaux-Arts School and to welcome the advent of the Bauhaus. This was not the godless direction that forced this great movement out of its country of origin. Indeed, it was God Himself who prompted Mies van der Rohe to utter the classic dictum, "God is in the details."

But when the new "schools" and their adherents forsook two millennia of "styles" and "neo-styles" and strove to imprint the whole works with their own "international" and "Organic" and "Brutal" styles, they too, guided by an unseeing hand, became obsolete.

And once again, the horizon and the countryside are enlivened by new forms, new expressions, new creations with which to honor the Creator. Thank God for that too!

Resurrection of a Viking ship

Unitarian Church
10 Lyons Plain Road, Westport, Connecticut 06880

Completed in 1964   **Victor Lundy, architect**

Services: Sunday, 10:30 a.m.
Seating Capacity: 250 (400 with foyer opened).
Open to visitors: Monday to Friday, 9 a.m. to 4 p.m. (office).
Telephone: (203) 227-7205
Construction Cost: $259,478
How to get there: Take Exit 42 from the Merritt Parkway and go north on Route 57 (Weston Road) for one mile. Turn right onto Lyons Plain Road. The church is two hundred yards down on the right.

Architect: **Lundy, Victor Alfred.** FAIA. Born in New York City, New York in 1923. Lundy was educated at Harvard University. Works represented: Westport Unitarian Church and Hartford Unitarian Church, both in Connecticut. Other important works: Residential, commercial, industrial, religious, educational, recreational and government buildings throughout the United States and also Latin America and the Middle East. Lundy has been visiting lecturer at Yale, Harvard, Columbia, Berkeley and other educational centers. He has received numerous awards, including Awards of Merit and First Honor Awards for the two Connecticut churches represented.

224

Unitarian Church; Westport, Connecticut

First Unitarian Congregational Society Church; Hartford, Connecticut

A mountain in suspension

First Unitarian Congregational Society Church
50 Bloomfield Avenue, Hartford, Connecticut 06105

Completed in 1951   **Victor Lundy, architect**

Services: September to June, Sunday, 10:30 a.m.
Seating Capacity: 350
Open to visitors: Daily, 9 a.m. to 3 p.m
Telephone: (203) 233-9897
Construction Cost: $650,000
How to get there: Go west from Hartford on Asylum Avenue to Scarborough Avenue (which is identified by a center esplenade; the Roman Catholic spires are visible on the left). Turn right onto Scarborough, and go to the end of the street. Turn left, and go about a mile to Bloomfield Avenue. The Unitarian Meetinghouse is in the broad valley on the right.

Architect: **Lundy, Victor** (see page 224).

Is it a fountain frozen in time and space? The canopy over a Tabernacle?

Church of the Blessed Sacrament, East Hartford – 1972
St. Peter Claver Church, West Hartford – 1969

Two Roman Catholic churches in the Greater Hartford area, when viewed as a pair, represent a fascinating exercise in similarities, contrasts, and contradictions. Though united in their expression of an identical liturgy, they are widely removed by differences in their individual vernacular.

The Church of the Blessed Sacrament and St. Peter Claver Church were designed by the same West Hartford-based architectural firm. Both are based on the same one-hundred-foot square plan, and both were erected in an eighteen-month period.

The two churches conform, naturally, to the same strict liturgical requirements and at the same time respond imaginatively to the freedom implicit in the new Roman Catholic liturgy. But here the similarities cease. Although the two churches are united in ritual, they represent the two extremes of the economic scale, and are separated sociologically by far more than the river that flows between them.

Church of the Blessed Sacrament; East Hartford, Connecticut

Saint Peter Claver Roman Catholic Church; West Hartford, Connecticut

Square, but in floor plan only

Church of the Blessed Sacrament

36 Cambridge Drive, East Hartford, Connecticut 06118

Completed in October, 1971   **Russell, Gibson, von Dohlen, Inc.,
architect**

The East Hartford Church is, in a superficial sense, the more "modern" of the two. It is an anonymous rectangular block without the usual identifying tower or spire. It is situated in an industrial area populated with tiny white clapboard bungalows, just out of reach of the shadow of the Pratt & Whitney Aircraft plant.

The floor plan is a flexible, open square, designed for quick and easy transformation from a place of divine worship to an area of secular activity. The concept recalls the early New England dual-purpose meetinghouse which was often square in plan, and of which Hingham's Old Ship Meetinghouse is an excellent example. (The Holy City, well documented and dimensioned in the Revelation of St. John, is also square in plan though its volume, with no exegetical clues to date, closely resembles a cube.)

The main feature of Blessed Sacrament Church is the surprisingly flexible character of the interior. Its excellent proportions are dominated by the most sophisticated of modern structural systems, the steel space frame. In its context, this feature is surprising, but not incongruous. It possesses an abstract purity, and a feeling of lightness and security that owes nothing to history. It is marred only by the spiral imprint of the cardboard forms on the surface of the supporting concrete columns. On the other hand, it would have gladdened the heart of Abbot Suger, who was the inspiration for the first truly Gothic church. The rhythmic pattern of the structural members, hung with multicolored banners, are the modern counterpart of the vaulted ceilings of Henry VII Chapel in Westminster Abbey and King's College Chapel in Cambridge.

Gone forever are the narthex, side aisles, sanctuary and ambulatory of the past. Instead, we have a basic square relieved by the freeform enclosures that form the vestibule. One houses the sacristy, the other a chapel for weekday devotions. The latter is distinguished by an altar with a beautiful antependium in carved wood.

The pastor, the Reverend James Harrison, informed me that "We wanted an all-purpose church." Judging by the vibrant atmosphere that

How far removed is this interior from Hingham's Old Ship Meetinghouse?

envelops this unique structure throughout the week, Blessed Sacrament is an architectural triumph.

Services: Sunday, 8, 9, 10:15, and 11:30 a.m.; Monday, 7:30 p.m.; Tuesday to Saturday, 9 a.m.

Seating Capacity: 500

Open to visitors: By appointment.

Telephone: (203) 568-2747

Construction Cost: $420,000

How to get there: Take I-84 east past Hartford, and exit at Route 2. Go about 2 miles to Exit 5B; go under Route 2 to the church.

Architect: **Russell, Gibson, von Dohlen, Inc.** The firm was founded in 1954 and is located in Farmington, Connecticut. Works represented: Blessed Sacrament Roman Catholic Church, East Hartford, Connecticut and St. Peter Claver Roman Catholic Church, West Hartford, Connecticut. Other important works: major structures for Aetna, Hallmark, Heublein, Pratt and Whitney, Scovill and United Technologies Corporations, among others, as well as banks, schools, community centers, churches, and residences throughout Connecticut and Massachusetts. This firm has been the recipient of many national and state awards and citations including the two churches represented.

231

Square, but in floor plan only

Saint Peter Claver Roman Catholic Church

47 Pleasant Street, West Hartford, Connecticut 06107

Completed on December 24, 1968   **Russell, Gibson, von Dohlen, Inc.**
architect

The West Hartford church makes the identical liturgical statement with a totally different architectural vocabulary.

St. Peter Claver Church is situated in a grove of shade trees surrounded by residences of varying taste on generously-zoned sites, all of which are the combined signature of upper-middle class opulence.

The structure recalls the "organic" vocabulary that Frank Lloyd Wright introduced a half-century ago. It is a handsome blend of architecture and natural elements. The rough fieldstone walls are laid with as much freedom as precision; the natural wood is stained rather than painted. The shaggy shingled roof sweeps upward in a gesture of devotion and simultaneously invites the light of day and of the Spirit to the interior through unseen skylights.

The exterior is pleasantly harmonious; the interior is profoundly startling. The pattern of ponderous wood girders bound together by iron gusset-plates studded with bolts suggest a Piranesi etching. It is as though, in the well-endowed suburbs of Hartford, one had entered a mighty medieval fortress or a very early Christian church minus the distinctive clerestory. The pastor and congregation have consciously eschewed the structural daring and psychological freedom of contemporary structural engineering and have opted for a return to the heavy, dark, and essentially safe and reassuring Romanesque. The whole exudes an atmosphere of unquestioned tradition of tested and accepted forms and materials, and is the symbol of solidity and security.

And yet the effect of the interior is not one of heaviness. The massive girders, silhouetted against the light that filters through the nine skylights, are separated from the supporting walls by a band of indirect lighting and rather than weigh upon them, seem to hover over the entire enclosure.

The interior of the church is a clearly phrased statement. The congregation has chosen to avoid the entrapment of novelty; it is not oblivious to the current trends in church design, but rather superior to them.

The individual liturgical elements are carefully selected and exquisitely detailed. The heavy oak-paneled entrance doors are repeated

This church is the embodiment of Martin Luther's "Mighty Fortress".

through the interior. The abstract patterns of the chipped glass are a millennium in advance of the realism of the same material in St. Joseph's Cathedral. The delicately poised crucifix recalls the suspended sculpture over the altar in the Rhode Island's Portsmouth Priory (see page 131).

The Church of St. Peter Claver is a rare experience in restraint, in exclusiveness, in quality without ostentation, in pride without vanity, and in impeccable taste. It is neither haughty nor humble. It belongs as much to the past as to the present. Perhaps its timeliness is its most important dimension.

Services: Sunday, 7:30, 9, 10:15, and 11:30 a.m.; Monday to Friday, 6:30 a.m.; Saturday, 8 a.m. and 5:30 p.m.

Seating Capacity: 700

Open to visitors: Daily to 6 p.m.

Telephone: (203) 521-2376

Construction Cost: Approximately $450,000.

How to get there: Follow Farmington Avenue west through the center of West Hartford. About three-quarters of a mile beyond the center, turn left at Pleasant Street.

Architect: **Russell, Gibson, von Dohlen, Inc.** (see page 231).

An Architectural Anomaly

When comparing these two churches, the natural reaction is to attribute the difference in visual effect to a significant difference in cost. The difference (excluding the cost of land in each case) is not surprising, but it is the reverse of what one would expect!

The fashionable edifice in West Hartford is listed at $24. per square foot. The East Hartford structure, on the other side of the tracks and of the Connecticut River as well, is given at $28.40.

Judging by the hand finishes, the special materials, and the air of luxury in St. Peter Claver Church, on the one hand, and the mass-produced elements, the standard processes, and the economy implicit in Blessed Sacrament Church on the other, the relative bottom-line figures are difficult to explain.

The obvious discrepancy cannot be attributed solely to the vagaries of the bidding procedure. The two churches were completed well before the period of rising costs and both within the operating range of the same general contractors. And surely when the cost of labor and materials are such vital factors in building today, there must, in each case, have been a fixed budget. How then can one explain that for two structures representing the extremes in the economic scale, the figures on the bottom line were the reverse of what one would expect?

This apparent contradiction can only be interpreted as the direct result of the process of architecture in the hands of gifted practitioners. The two churches are the result of calculated analysis, by the architect, of all the factors involved in the two problems.

The same architect, or two competing architects, faced with two superficially similar problems, might conceivably have produced identical designs. History is not lacking in graphic instances of this approach.

Here the solutions were made in terms of the specific communities in diametrically opposed contexts. The key was the special regard, by the architect, for the character of the two congregations and their vastly different physical environments. The guiding motive was the solution, and not the cost factor.

One has only to imagine how pretentious and foreign St. Peter Claver would have been in the shadow of Route 2, or how jarring, to use a classic understatement, to come upon Blessed Sacrament on Pleasant Street! As they stand, however, the two solutions seem eminently appropriate and fitting, and the cost, when measured in terms of the enthusiasm and numbers of their respective parishioners, totally irrelevant. They are parallel examples of what great architecture, in its disregard for the obvious, is all about.

Saint Matthew's Episcopal Church/Wilton Presbyterian Church; Wilton, Connecticut

Two in one

Saint Matthew's Episcopal Church
Wilton Presbyterian Church
Wolfpit Road, Wilton, Connecticut 06897

Completed in 1971   **Willis N. Mills, Jr., architect**

The two-sanctuary complex in Wilton, Connecticut, is a unique creation.

First, this unusual combination of two religious structures is a striking visual composition. The abstract trigonometry of its varied forms,
each one reflecting an aspect of the ensemble's many functions, is an
esthetic triumph. Hidden within a wooded enclosure, it is at the same
time a challenge and a complement to its environment. The juxtaposition of solids and resulting voids seems to change constantly with the
position of the sun and the viewpoint of the observer. And the descend-
ing volumes of this surprisingly organic unit appear to join the gently
sloping site in a formal yet loving relationship.

Secondly, there is literally nothing about this intrinsically religious

After three hundred years, we have come full circle. Whether by accident or by design, this white-walled, wood-beamed interior closely resembles the meetinghouse described at the beginning of this book. Is it "back to square one," or did we ever leave it?

structure that imposes an atmosphere of "religion" in the traditional sense. There is a refreshingly contemporary yet timeless anonymity in the design that is an open invitation to human fellowship, but that is all. This quality is best exemplified in the paved court that marks the center of the design. This is no classic atrium or medieval cloister. It is a frank and eloquent response to the clearly defined program which stated that two separate congregations wished to worship simultaneously – and carry on their separate activities as well – within a single structural frame.

The forthright solution to this problem is eminently satisfying. The massive element on the left of the court houses the Episcopalian sanctuary; a corresponding volume on the right encloses the Presbyterian all-purpose parish hall. Between these two, connecting and not separating them, are the lounges, classrooms, offices and other facilities necessary to the secondary activities of both groups.

The interior is a reflection of the exterior. Clear expanses of white-painted masonry combine harmoniously with stained natural wood and neutral carpeting. This building is not a self-conscious monument to its creators; it is a background, in every respect, for the activities of its inhabitants. There are only two low-keyed suggestions of what might be termed "traditional" features in the area of buildings dedicated to religion. One is the pair of tiny windows surmounted by pointed arches and glazed with colored glass, a fleeting echo of the atmosphere one automatically attributes to the era of the great cathedrals. The other is apparent in the pattern of the laminated wood struts in the ceiling of the Episcopalian sanctuary. Were the crossed beams actually required to ensure the stability of the skylight overhead? Or were they introduced to recall the saltire, or diagonal cross that legend associates with the crucifixion of St. Andrew, and which is the distinguishing feature of the original flag of Presbyterian Scotland? It is difficult to imagine that this understated touch of symbolism was introduced without specific intention.

The creation as a whole has been referred to as "ecumenical" which, strictly speaking, it is not. The union of two disparate persuasions under the same roof is less one of the spirit than of the body; it is not so much a marriage as a form of cohabitation. Perhaps, considering the healthy, animated atmosphere to which the entire structure is constant host, the better term to describe it is "symbiotic" in a mutually productive sense.

However, the masterful yet unpretentious design overrides these subjective considerations. The authority of its planes and volumes owes nothing to history nor to the transient present and commands the full respect of the entire profession. St. Matthew's Episcopal Parish is a masterpiece of restraint and understatement; it contains all those elusive elements that cannot be tabulated nor measured, but which can be unmistakably savored in the totality of a superior work of art.

Services: Sunday, 8 and 10 a.m.
Open to visitors: Apply to Secretary, Monday to Friday, 9 a.m. to 3 p.m.
Telephone: (203) 762-7400
Seating Capacity: 450
Construction Cost: Unknown.
How to get there: Take Exit 40 from the Merritt Parkway, and go north on Route 7 for about 4 miles to Wolfpit Road. Turn left, and follow the road for about 2 miles to a four-way stop at Belden Hill Road. The church is about 200 yards beyond on the right, in a grove of trees.

Architect: **Mills, Willis N. Jr., AIA.** Born in New York, New York in 1933. Mills was educated at Princeton University. He is a senior partner in the firm of SMS Architects, New Canaan, Connecticut. Work represented: St. Matthew's Episcopal, Wilton, Presbyterian Church, Wilton, Connecticut. Other important works: New Canaan Library, Tokeneke Club, Darien, and the Hudson River Museum in Yonkers, New York. Mills' firm has received National AIA Awards in 1975 and 1976.

Medieval

Wren-Georgian

Gibbs-Federal

Gothic Revival

Romanesque

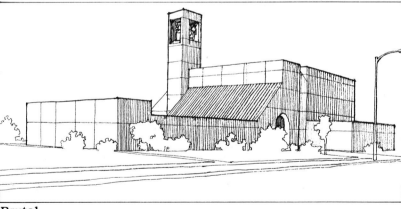

Brutal

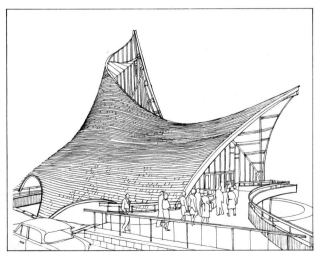

Emotional-Structural

Appendix A

Guide To The Architectural Styles

The Meetinghouse Period, 1640-1830

Phase 1.   Medieval–1640-1745

Phase 2.   Wren-Georgian–1730-1789

Phase 3.   Gibbs-Federal–1750-1830

The Revival Period, 1814-1930

Phase 4.   Classic–1820-1840

Phase 5.   Gothic Revival–1814-1930

Phase 6.   Romanesque–1870-1893

The Modern Period, 1930-present

Phase 7.   Organic

Phase 8.   International

Phase 9.   Emotional-Structural

Phase 10.   Brutal

Phase 11.   Post-Modern

The Meetinghouse Period

The Medieval Phase, c. 1640 through c. 1745

The earliest houses of worship in New England were not "churches" in the historic sense. The townspeople held their religious gatherings and their social and political gatherings as well in a "meetinghouse."

The first structures of this type were built of logs, with gable roofs covered with thatch. Early seventeenth-century Connecticut examples have been recorded in Middletown, Washington (then known as Judea), and Salisbury, but none has been preserved.

The demand for greater space, and perhaps for greater comfort and sophistication, led to a structure whose timber frame, secured by wooden pegs, was sheathed in clapboard. The modest gable roof was discarded for a pyramidal or "hipped" roof surmounted by a cupola and, more often than not, by a belfry.

Examples are referred to in the files of Milford, Hartford, New Haven and Wethersfield, but the single extant structure, a paradigm of this building type, is the Old Ship Meetinghouse in Hingham, Massachusetts (see page 3).

This unique creation was an American invention with no European precedent. For reasons of unity and community as well as for structural compactness, the floor plan was square. There were three entrances, the central one facing the pulpit. Earlier seating was on rude benches, with men on the preacher's right and women on his left. Later a system of partitioned cubicles, called "box pews," (or sometimes "sheep-pen pews") was introduced, large enough to accommodate entire families. Subscriptions to this seating arrangement were often the main source of building funds. Additional seating occurred in the second-level "galleries" which were located on three sides of the square facing the pulpit.

Windows were fairly large and glazed with diamond-shaped panes of handmade clear glass set into lead cames. There was no sculpture, no painting, no decoration of any kind except for the row of spindles that sometimes ornamented the partitions of the box-pews, and the rather ornate pulpit with its wood moldings, paneling and turned balustrades. The pulpit was raised, partly to maintain visibility from the gallery, but also to relieve the "clean Puritan austerity" (and utter monotony) of the interior. For the same reason the roof trusses were often left exposed, and doubtless the artists who fashioned the massive trusses were not averse to displaying evidence of their superb craftsmanship.

The typical early Colonial meetinghouse was a single large room, sometimes fifty feet square. This was called variously the "auditorium," the "Audience Room," or the "Sanctuary." There was no vestry, no vestibule, and no "Helas," ("No rest rooms!" to quote the custodian of the medieval cathedral of Auxerre in France.) These factors did not prevent this building type from appearing as late as 1730 in Connecticut.

240

New England's "medieval" meetinghouse appeared a half-millenium after the Romanesque monasteries and Gothic cathedrals of medieval Europe.

The hand-hewn roof trusses of Hingham's meetinghouse were raised into position two years after Charles LeBrun began the interior of Versailles' Galerie des Glaces and six years after Christopher Wren began the construction of St. Paul's Cathedral in London.

In 1688, when tiny diamond-shaped panes of glass finally replaced oiled paper in New England, plate glass in large sheets appeared, to reflect the images of Louis XIV and his coterie of effete courtiers.

While the Puritan preacher, accompanied, at best, by the flute and the bass viol, "lined out" the hymns before his congregation, the world of music gave birth, in 1689, to Domenico Scarlatti, George Frederick Handel and Johann Sebastian Bach.

And while the New England family huddled around the wood-burning fireplace and feasted, on rare occasions, on pumpkin and apple pie, the continent of Europe relished a dessert later to be known as "ice cream."

The Wren-Georgian Phase, 1730 through 1789

A significant change in the layout and outward appearance of the Colonial meetinghouse took place early in the eighteenth century. Inspired in part by the "Great Awakening" and the accompanying demand for greater seating space, the square plan was broadened into a rectangle. The pulpit was located at the center of one of the long sides, opposite the principle entrance. Otherwise the interior remained the same as in the medieval period. Outside, the hipped roof was abandoned in favor of the gable, and in many cases the belfry was omitted from the ridge.

Examples of this aspect of the Wren-Georgian phase, all built between 1738 and 1789, may still be seen in Rockingham, Vermont, Amesbury, Massachusetts, and in Salem and Sandown, New Hampshire. A superb example exists in Alna, Maine. (See page 111.)

Improved communications with Great Britain led to the addition of a novel and distinctive feature. In response to the human desire for embellishment, a tower with a spire was added at one end. In order to achieve the vertical effect of Gothic architecture, Christopher Wren had introduced this feature in his City of London churches after the Great Fire of 1666.

This nonliturgical element became the architectural signature of the Colonial meetinghouse until the American Revolution. The prime examples are Old South Meetinghouse in Boston, Trinity Church in Newport, and Wethersfield and Farmington Congregational Churches in Connecticut. All are described in detail in the text of this book.

It is interesting to note that the departure from the square plan was not entirely due to structural considerations. Old South in Boston, built in 1729 is a ninety-four foot by 67-foot rectangle, but First Baptist in Providence, erected a half century later, is eighty-foot square in plan.

The modest Wren-Georgian structures seemed to act as a shield between their occupants and the outside world.

Certainly there was no apparent communication between the simple wooden boxes of the period and the imposing brick Capitol and the stately Governor's Mansion in Williamsburg, both completed two decades before Boston's Old South Church.

Culturally and philosophically, the meetinghouse was far more than a mere decade removed from the massive pretensions of Blenheim Palace, erected in 1720 and several light years distant from the magnificent Jesuit-inspired Rococo churches of south Germany.

Although transatlantic postal service was instituted in 1724, the Congregationalists, the Presbyterians and the Episcopalians were carefully insulated from Voltaire's radical views on religion and the popularity of Hogarth's *Rake's Progress.*

On the other hand, the diurnal demands of the New England climate must have helped to preserve them from entrapment by the South Sea Bubble and the disastrous financial manipulations of John Law.

And whatever time the Puritans could glean from their domestic preoccupations must have been absorbed in coping simultaneously with the French, the Indians, and the British.

The Gibbs-Federal Phase, 1750 through 1830

Political independence, economic prosperity, and the growing tendency toward the separation between Church and State were factors accompanying the creation of the third meetinghouse type. But none of these approaches the impact of the publication of two books.

The first, entitled *The Book of Architecture,* and consisting wholly of engravings by the London architect, James Gibbs, was published in 1726 and reached the colonies by mid-century. The engravings are the work of "E. Kirkall, sculp." who credits the designs, with a late-Renaissance flourish, to "Jacobo Gibbs, Architecto." The second "The Country Builder's Assistant" was illustrated by Asher Benjamin, architect from Greenfield, Massachusetts, and appeared in 1797.

These two seminal works were studied by artisans, master-builders and gentleman-architects throughout the newly-founded Republic and the result was a giant step forward in American religious architecture. This change, like the previous one, was not due to structural or liturgical considerations. Except for the fact that the pulpit was now located at the narrow end of a rectangle, the interior, including the gallery, remained as it was in the previous phase.

But the tower that Wren had located rising from the ground was now set astride the ridge, over the main entrance, establishing a relation which did not exist in the typical Wren-type churches, as in Farmington. (see page 139.)

The facade was then further accented by a totally non-utilitarian yet highly impressive Classic portico.

The adroit combination of these three elements can clearly be traced to James Gibbs' masterful design for St. Martin-in-the-Fields in London, the design of which is one of the features of Gibbs' book. It is easy to see how a pleasing combination of classic elements flattered and impressed a society where contacts with Classic and Renaissance architecture were minimal at best.

Examples are to be found throughout New England, especially in Connecticut. The style spread out to Niagara-on-the-Lake in Canada, to Talmadge, Ohio, and to St. Michael's Church in Charleston, South Carolina, erected, surprisingly, in 1752 through 1761. And of utmost importance, the precursor of the Gibbs-Federal style in New England is Providence's First Baptist Church. (see page 125.)

Asher Benjamin's *Design for a Church* (see illustration) though appearing later, had somewhat less impact. Congregational churches in Middlebury (see page 85) and Bennington (see page 83), both in Vermont, are good examples of this secondary aspect of the Gibbs-Federal phase.

The Classic Phase (or Greco-Roman), 1820 through 1840

Thomas Jefferson, architect and our third president, was almost single-handedly responsible for the introduction of Roman Revival architecture to this country. Through the impact of his personality, his energy, and his erudition, almost every nineteenth-century city and town is distinguished today by at least one important structure in either the Roman style, with its Corinthian capitals and its domes, or its neo-Greek counterpart with Doric columns and pediment.

The nation's Capitol is a grand climax to a trend in revival architecture that outlasted any other. The Roman-inspired architecture preceded the Greek. In the ecclesiastical field the outstanding monument is Baltimore's Pantheon-inspired Roman Catholic cathedral, designed by English-born Benjamin Latrobe and completed in 1804.

The Greek revival emerged upon the American scene a generation later. Somewhat more reserved and refined, though often almost undistinguishable from the Roman, this style endured until 1920 when the Lincoln Memorial in Washington climaxed a grand city plan and a grand epoch.

New England, however, has little to show in the field of Classic churches, either Greek or Roman. Perhaps the lone example worth noting is the First Church of Quincy, Massachusetts labelled the "Stone Temple," built of granite, and donated by John Adams. Both he and his son, John Quincy Adams, are buried within its walls.

Classic architecture lacked the individuality of the Federal style, and was soon supplanted by the neo-Gothic.

The Revival Period

The Gothic Revival Style, 1814 through 1930

ORIGINS: Episcopalian clergymen, responding to the growing demand for more space (and for architectural individuality) urged their architects to adopt the style that had persisted in England since the twelfth century.

The Gothic style was given renewed life through the influence of the author Horace Walpole, who designed his "Gothick" retreat, "Strawberry Hill," in Twickenham in 1776. Authors and architects of the "Romantic Period" gave the style further legitimacy. In fact, the program for the 1840 competition for London's Houses of Parliament made the design in Gothic style mandatory.

Although the Federal styles continued to appear sporadically, the neo-Gothic swept the entire country and persisted, particularly in and near the New England area, until 1930.

CHARACTERISTICS: Columns, pediments and all the standard neo-classic details, including the Palladian window, were abandoned in favor of the pointed arch, the vaulted ceiling, the buttress and stained glass window. The change was actually a Renaissance in reverse.

The exterior was more often than not in masonry, although the veneer of prosperity soon gave way to wood in the "Board-and-Batten" version of Gothic in mid-century.

The neo-Gothic church was at first a strictly Episcopalian product. It was soon adopted by all denominations, however, and examples in both materials may be seen throughout the entire United States.

EXAMPLES:
Outside New England:
Trinity Episcopal Church
    New York, 1846, Richard Upjohn, architect.
St. Patrick's Cathedral
    New York, 1858-1879, James Renwick, architect.
National Episcopalian Cathedral
    Washington, D.C.; Vaughn and Bodley, architects, begun in 1907, still unfinished.

New England:
Trinity Church, Episcopal
    New Haven, 1814, Ithiel Town, architect.
Christ Church Episcopal Cathedral
    Hartford, Connecticut, 1827, Ithiel Town, architect.

First Parish
  Brunswick, Maine, 1846, Richard Upjohn, architect
Holy Cross R.C. Church
  Holyoke, Massachusetts, 1928, James Donahue, architect
St. Mary's Church
  Stamford, Connecticut, 1928, Shaw & O'Connell, architects.

(All the New England churches are described in the text. See general index.)

The Romanesque Style, 1870 through 1893

ORIGIN: The distinctive religious form that appeared quite suddenly on America's eastern horizon late in the nineteenth century was the work of Boston's Henry Hobson Richardson. But for his imagination, energy and individuality, this Harvard-educated and Beaux-Arts-oriented genius might have followed the well-worn footsteps of his eclectic-minded colleagues.

Instead, his precedent-shattering designs spread throughout the country for two decades, and he is acknowledged as the first American architect to achieve international acclaim.

CHARACTERISTICS: Richardson's assertive style is a clear departure from the neo-Gothic that prevailed in the 1870s. The materials are rough-faced local stone and clay-tile roofs. The major design elements are low, heavy round arches resting on short, sturdy pillars. There are often massive square towers, sometimes decorated with turrets at each corner. The whole suggests authority rather than grace, simplicity rather than elegance, and above all, security and permanence.

Richardson-Romanesque, as it soon became known, owed little to the already firmly-implanted Tuscan, the Lombard, the Italianate, and nothing at all to the Second Empire style, which it replaced. However, the details and massing of this new idiom clearly recall the Romanesque of Southern France and Spain.

Oddly enough, the parade of the styles is again the reverse of the historical pattern. American Romanesque followed rather than preceded the Gothic, much as the Greek Revival followed rather than preceded the neo-Roman. Its impact was profound throughout the whole range of building types. Today's typical eastern town, for example, might possess a Federal-style church, a neo-Classic bank and a museum, a Gothic church and perhaps a small university. But it would almost certainly possess a library in Richardson's style, as well as several major residences, an office building, a railroad station, an armory and a jail in the same unmistakable vernacular.

Richardson died at the age of forty-eight. He did not live to see his eponymous style replaced, through the influence of Richard Morris

Hunt, by the neo-Roman revival as expressed in Chicago's Columbia Exposition in 1893.

EXAMPLES: Boston's Trinity Episcopal Church (see page 39) is the definitive proof of Richardson's genius. This church followed by a half decade the erection of Boston's Brattle Street Church (see page 34).

The Modern Period, 1930 to present

The special character of all twentieth century (after 1930) architecture was the result of the reaction against the century-old influence of France's Ecole des Beaux Arts. The movement was spearheaded in America by Frank Lloyd Wright and almost simultaneously, in Europe, by adherents of Germany's Bauhaus School.

CHARACTERISTICS: New forms and materials were added to the design vocabulary; the liturgy throughout the denominations was re-analyzed in terms of plan, acoustics, air conditioning, landscaping, and the economics of building. And during Vatican II, the now almost-legendary Pope John XXIII gave his *aedeficatur* to a new physical rapprochement between the congregation and the ministry.

But the most important single element that binds together all the various manifestations of the period is the greatly increased importance of the architect himself. The desire to give substance, in contemporary terms, to the age-old mystery of communal worship is now filtered through the mind, the heart, and the hand of the individual designer.

For this reason, the resulting rich conglomeration of new religious expressions all but defies classification. In general, however, churches of America (and especially in New England), built after World War II, fall generally into one of five categories described briefly as follows:

Organic

Natural local materials in great variety, weathered and often unfinished. A special feature is made of allying the interior with the exterior and thus, along with natural landscaping, relating the building to its immediate environment. The style was first made popular through the work and writings of Frank Lloyd Wright. Notable New England example, St. Peter Claver Roman Catholic Church, West Hartford, Connecticut. (see page 232).

International

Geometric, modular, rigid, most often in steel and glass. Carefully studied, often "classic" proportions, but sometimes resulting in a dehumanized appearance. Rough materials are avoided, and relationship to the site is not stressed. This style was promulgated by the Bauhaus School of Germany, one of whose founders, Walter Gropius, migrated to Cambridge, Massachusetts in 1937, and whose colleague, Ludwig Mies van der Rohe, came to Chicago in 1938. Best New England example, Blessed Sacrament Roman Catholic Church, East Hartford, Connecticut. (see page 230).

Emotional-Structural

A development of the Organic style, but free of its geometrical limitations. Free form in plan, section and elevation, but still strictly functional in construction. The outstanding work of Eero Saarinen falls into this classification. Great variety of materials, as well as ingenious structural experimentation. Best New England example, United Church, Rowayton, Connecticut. (see page 211.)

Brutal

Architecture as sculpture, both in form and in surface. The term is related to the work of Switzerland's Le Corbusier, whose chapel at Ronchamp in France is the outstanding church of this century. A New England example: St. Paul's Cathedral in Burlington, Vermont. (see page 95.)

Post-Modern

From the mid-seventies, the church has been all but submerged in the shadow of the skyscraper, the corporate headquarters, the sports complex and the shopping plaza. The architect, meanwhile, has become aware of the limited vocabulary of the Organic and the Emotional Structural styles on the one hand, and the painful lack of human expression inherent in the International and the Brutal styles.

Frank Lloyd Wright's architectural Jeremiad, "A finger pointing toward God" was spiritually unconvincing; Le Corbusier's "A house is a machine for living" (and its implicit corollary relating to the church), and Mies van der Rohe's "Less is more" were emotionally unsatisfactory in relation to a belief in a personal deity.

Now, in the early eighties, the architect is attempting to reestablish contact with his client by making an eclectic reassessment of the foregoing half-century of "Modern" architecture, and then adding a nostalgic acknowledgment of the human element expressed in the historic styles. The combination has been the subject of some debate. However, the Eiffel Tower, with its Baroque profiles and details, was violently rejected by the critic of its day and, for all we know, so were the Parthenon, Santa Sophia, and the Abbey of St. Denis. In the end, it is time, as well as man, that is the measure of all things.

Except for Rev. Robert Schuler's (and architect Philip Johnson's) Crystal Cathedral in Garden Grove, California, and Wilton's Ecumenical Center (see page 235), the erection of churches in this phase is highly restrained at best. This may be the age's tacit appraisal of itself as well as of its architecture.

Appendix B
Churches Listed On The National Register Of Historic Places

Additional Listings:

NHL: Designated as a National Historic Landmark

HABS: Recorded by the Historic American Building Survey

G: Recipient of National Park Service Grant-in-Aid for Historic Preservation

Massachusetts:
Hingham, Old Ship Meetinghouse, **NHL, HABS, G**
Boston, Christ Church (Old North Church), **NHL, HABS, G**
Boston, St. Stephen's Church
Boston, Old South Church, **NHL, HABS, G**
Boston, King's Chapel, **NHL**
Boston, Park Street Church
Boston, Old West Church, **NHL, HABS**
Boston, First Baptist Church
Boston, Trinity Church, **NHL**
Lancaster, First Unitarian Church, **NHL, HABS, G**

Vermont:
Richmond, Round Church, **G**
Bennington, First Congregational Church, **HABS**
Middlebury, Congregational Church
Burlington, First Unitarian Church, **HABS**

New Hampshire:
Peterborough, First Unitarian Church

Rhode Island:
Newport, Trinity Church, **NHL, HABS**
Newport, Touro Synagogue, **HABS**
Providence, First Baptist Church, **NHL, HABS**

Maine:
Wiscasset, Alna Meetinghouse, **HABS**
Brunswick, First Parish Church

Connecticut:
Wethersfield, First Church of Christ, **HABS**
Farmington, First Church, **NHL**
Brooklyn, First Church
Brooklyn, Old Trinity Church
Cheshire, First Congregational
Litchfield, First Congregational, **HABS**
Guilford, First Congregational, **HABS**
Old Lyme, First Congregational, **G**
New Haven, United Church, **G**
New Haven, Center Church, **G**
New Haven, Trinity Church, **G**
Hartford, South Church
Hartford, Center Church

Glossary of Architectural Terms

Ambulatory. A corridor leading behind an altar from one side to the other.

Antependium. The front face of an altar.

Apse. The altar end of a church, usually semicircular in plan.

Arabesque. A decorative pattern of interlaced lines or bands in geometrical patterns.

Arch. A form of construction, usually of masonry, in which a number of units span an opening.

Ashlar. Masonry having a face of square or rectangular stones, in varying sizes.

Atelier. An artist's studio or architect's drafting-room where design is taught.

Atrium. The open-roofed court of a Roman dwelling.

Baldachino. A canopy supported or suspended over an altar. Also known as a "ciborium."

Baroque. A term applied to design in the late Renaissance period (from 1550 to 1700) in reaction against Classical form, characterized by elaboration of scrolls, curves, and carved ornaments. From "Barocco," Portuguese for a faulty pearl, but also possibly from Frederico Barucci, Italian architect of the period.

Baluster. A pillar or column supporting a handrail, a series of such being called a balustrade.

Basilica. An unusually large church, not a cathedral.

Belfry. A small bell tower, nearly always a part of a building.

Belt course. A flat, horizontal member of relatively slight projection, marking a division in the wall plane.

Board-and-Batten. A term applied to the all-wood architecture of the late nine-teenth century in which many details were derived from Gothic architecture. From the French "baton," stick.

Braces. Any oblique member set to hold steady one of the principal members of a frame or truss.

Brutal. Name given to the style originated by the Swiss architect Le Corbusier, characterized by a highly sculptural form and unfinished concrete surfaces.

Buttress. An abutting pier which strengthens a wall, sometimes taking the thrust of an inner arch.

Byzantine. A style of architecture that had its beginnings about four centuries B.C. and still persists, especially in the Orthodox Church. Characterized by domes on "pendentives" or spherical triangles, and decorated with mosaics. From Byzantium, the city which became Constantinople, capitol of the Roman Empire in 324 A.D. and renamed Istanbul in 1453 A.D.

Cames. A soft-metal division strip between adjacent pieces of glass in leaded or stained-glass windows.

Campanile. A bell tower.

Capital. The top member or group of members of a column, pier, shaft, or pilaster.

Carillon. A set of bells tuned to musical intervals and arranged to be played as an instrument.

Catacombs. Subterranean vaults or excavations in rock, used for burial.

Chancel. That portion of a church interior containing the altar and reserved for clergy and choir, and mainly for Episcopal churches.

Choir Stall. Divisions with fixed seats for the clergy and choir, often elaborately carved.

Clerestory. An upper stage in a building with windows above adjacent roofs.

Classic. A term referring to Greek and Roman art, but sometimes used to designate anything of the highest rank or class.

Cloister. A paved and sheltered passageway, usually along the walls of an enclosed court, and open on one side.

Coffer. A recessed panel in a flat or vaulted ceiling.

Colonnade. A row of columns with their entablatures.

Colonnette. A small column of secondary use.

Corinthian. Third of the three major Greek "Orders" of architecture in which the capitals of columns are decorated with acanthus leaves. This type of capital is used more frequently in Roman than in Greek architecture.

Cornice. The upper portion of the entablature, also used as the term for any crowning projection.

Cove. A concave molding. The curved junction between a ceiling and side wall, above a cornice if there is one.

Crocket. In Gothic architecture a projecting block or spur of stone carved with foliage.

Cross section. The representation of an object as it would appear if cut away to reveal the internal arrangement or structure.

Cupola. A terminal structure, square or round in plan, rising above a main roof.

Dolmen. A burial chamber of prehistoric times.

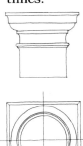

Doric. The simplest of the three principal classical "Orders" in which the capitals of columns are a simple curved molding under a shallow square block, as in the Parthenon of Athens.

Elevations. A graphic projection, at a given scale and upon a vertical plane, of an object, such as the exterior faces of a building.

Esplanade. A concourse or landscaped plateau with drives and walks.

Entablature. In classical architecture, the horizontal group of members immediately above the column capitals; divided into three major parts, it consists of architrave, frieze, and cornice.

Facade. A face of building, usually the front.

Faceted glass. Same as Chunk Glass, or "chipped glass," usually one inch or more in thickness, as opposed to ordinary stained glass, which is usually approximately one-eighth of an inch in thickness.

Federal. An American style following the Georgian and preceding the Classic Revival. Used in residences, churches and public buildings; principal exponent, Charles Bulfinch. Approximately 1789-1820.

Fenestration. The disposition of windows in a facade.

Filigree. Intricate, delicate, or fanciful ornamentation.

Finial. A terminal form at the top of spire, gable, gateway, or pinnacle.

Fleche. A slender spire, usually over the intersection of nave and transept axes.

Fluted. Decorated with parallel, semicircular grooves, as in a Classic column.

Flying Buttress. A masonry prop that springs from a pier or other support and abuts against another part of the structure to resist thrust.

Folie, folly. A costly but useless structure built to satisfy the whim of some eccentric and thought to show his folly.

Fresco. The term originally applied to painting on a wall while the plaster is wet, but is often used for any wall painting not in oil colours.

Frieze. A band member in the vertical plane, sometimes decorated with sculpture relief, occurring just under a cornice.

Gazebo. An open pavilion built for a view.

Georgian. A term applied to Late Renaissance English architecture circa 1702-1830. Best U.S. examples: Williamsburg, Westover, and Carter's Grove in Virginia.

Gingerbread. The name given to the style of American residential architecture in wood, appearing after 1860, and characterized by overly rich scroll-saw ornamentation. Closely resembling the self-explanatory "Steamboat Gothic" style, and sometimes referred to as the "Jigsaw style."

Gothic. The style of architecture developed from the twelfth to the fifteenth centuries, characterized by the ribbed vault, the flying buttress, and the pointed arch.

Gusset-plates. A triangular piece stiffening an angular meeting of two or more members in a framework.

Gynaeceum. The women's section of a Greek dwelling.

Hammer-beam. A short beam projecting from an interior wall and, as a cantilever, supporting one end of an arch timber.

Helical. Resembling a flat spiral form or rising structure; also referring to the volute of the Ionic capital.

Hipped roof. Has sloped instead of vertical ends.

Iconostasis. In the Greek Church, a screen corresponding to the altar rail in other churches.

International. A term designating the architectural style developed by the Bauhaus School and culminating in the work of Ludwig Mies van der Rohe.

Ionic. The second of the three Greek "orders." Its capitals are recognized by the scrolls or "volutes" at the far corner. Used throughout the White House in Washington, D.C.

Keystone. The wedge-shaped top member of an arch.

Laminated. Made up of thin layers, as plywood or laminated structural members.

Late Georgian. See Federal style.

Lintel. The horizontal member of the most common structural form—a beam resting its two ends under separate posts.

Lodge. The medieval term for the mason's workshop and living-quarters, set up when a church, castle, or house was to be built.

Lombard. An architectural style developed in Italy between the sixth and thirteenth centuries. Also termed Italian Romanesque.

Maitre d'oeuvre. Construction superintendent, and often chief designer as well, in France in the Middle Ages.

Moat. A trench surrounding a defense wall.

Modillion. A bracket form used in series.

Molding. The contours given to projecting members.

Monolithic. A single block of stone or concrete in or for a structure.

Mosaic. Decorative surfaces formed by small cubes of stone, glass, and marble.

Mullion. A dividing member between panes of glass in a door or window.

Narthex. The entrance vestibule of a church.

Nave. That portion of a church interior on the main axis, and not including the transepts, for the occupation of the lay worshippers.

Nimbus. A circular halo.

Norman. The architecture of Normandy, but more particularly the English variation of Romanesque after the Norman conquest in 1066 A.D.

Oculus. The circular opening occasionally formed at the top of a dome.

Ogival. Derived from *ogive*, French for the "rib" in French Gothic vaulting. The term was applied to Gothic architecture until the Renaissance when the critic Vasari implanted the style with its present and intentionally pejorative designation.

Ogive. A diagonal rib of simple vaulting

intersection. French term for pointed arch. The adjective is "ogival."

Organic. According to Random House Dictionary: " . . . having a structure and a plan that fulfill perfectly the functional requirements of the building (as in plant and animal forms) and that form in themselves an intellectually lucid integrated whole." A term popularized by the architect Frank Lloyd Wright and applied to his work and his philosophy.

Parvis. The open space in front of and around cathedrals and churches; a corruption of "Paradise."

Pavilion. A temporary or movable shelter, sometimes merely a tent; a small outbuilding.

Pediment. The triangular face of a roof gable, especially in its classical form.

Pendentive. A triangular segment of vaulting used to effect a transition at the angles from a square or polygon base to a dome above. See "Byzantine architecture."

Piazza. In Italy, an open space or public square in a city.

Pier. An upright structure of masonry to serve as a principal support, whether isolated or part of a wall.

Pilaster. An engaged pier or column of shallow depth.

Pile. A columnar support that is driven into the ground as part of a foundation.

Pinnacle. A terminal ornament or protecting cap, usually tapered upward to a point or knob.

Place. An open rectangular space in a community. (French).

Platz. An open rectangular space in a community. (German)

Plaza. An open rectangular space in a community. (Spanish)

Polyhedron. Having several similar faces.

Porch. A roofed space outside the main walls of a building and at an entrance.

Portico. An entrance porch.

Post-tensioned. Reinforced concrete in which the reinforcing steel rods are stretched to their ultimate strength after the concrete is allowed to harden.

Premiated. Distinguished by an award of merit in competition.

Prestressed. Reinforced concrete in which the reinforcing steel rods are stretched to their ultimate strength before the concrete is allowed to "set," or harden.

Pre-Raphaelite. Name of a society founded in 1848 by the English painter Rosetti and others to advance the style and spirit of Italian painting before Raphael.

Quadrangle. A rectangular court bordered by a building or buildings.

Quoin. One of the corner stones of a wall when these are emphasized by size, by more formal cutting, by more conspicuous jointing, or by difference in texture.

Rake. A slope or inclination, as of a roof, gable, or stair string.

Reeded. A molding, or a surface, made up of closely spaced parallel, half-round, convex profiles.

Reredos. A screen forming a background for an altar.

Rococo. Sometimes referred to as "Late Baroque" whose characteristic is the Baroque carried to the extreme, particularly in a lavish use of curves and a great variety of materials. From "Rocaille," a shell-like form, 1700 through 1775.

Rib. A transverse or diagonal structural member of arched vaulting, usually emphasized.

Romanesque. A style "like the Roman" that made the transition from the Roman to the Gothic styles from the ninth to the twelfth centuries.

Rustication. A method of forming stonework with roughened surfaces and recessed joints.

Sacristy. A room where church vestments and sacred vessels are kept, and where the clergy robe. Used mainly in Roman Catholic churches.

Sanctuary. That part of a church where the principal altar is situated. Used mainly in Roman Catholic churches.

Sash. A frame for glass to close a window opening.

Soffit. The finished underside of a lintel, arch, or other spanning member, usually overhead.

Sounding-board. A reflector made of resonant material, set above and behind a pulpit, bandstand, or the like.

Space-frame. A form of roof construction, usually in steel or aluminum, in which the principle of the truss is utilized in three dimensions instead of two, thus creating a supporting structure out of the entire roof.

Spindle. A short turned part, as that on a baluster.

Spire. The tapering termination of a tower in Gothic or Renaissance architecture.

Square. An open rectangular space in a community.

Tabernacle. A house of worship. A receptacle for the consecrated elements of the Eucharist.

Tetrahedron. A three-dimensional object having four similar faces.

Tower. A tall structure, usually square or round in plan, rising to a greater height than its surroundings.

Tracery. The curving mullions of a stone window, as in Gothic architecture.

Transept. Either of the lateral arms in a church of cruciform plan.

Transom. An opening over a door or window, usually for ventilation, and containing a glazed or solid sash, usually hinged or pivoted. The horizontal division or cross-bar of a window.

Trapezoid. A two-dimensional surface having four or more sides.

Triforium. A gallery or range of arches above the side aisles or the longitudinal arches bounding nave or choir in a church.

Truss. A number of timbers framed together to bridge a space, to be self-supporting, and to carry other timbers.

Tympanum. The space enclosed by the three molded sides of a pediment, or by the lines of a semicircular overdoor panel or the like.

Urban design. The design of a group of structures with special consideration for the spaces around and in between the structures.

Vault. That part of a structure roofed by arched masonry.

Volute. A spiral ornament often used as a pair, as in the Ionic capital.

Vestry. A room in which ecclesiastical vestments, sacred vessels, and the like are stored, and in which the clergy and choristers robe for church services. Usually used in Episcopal churches.

Victorian. Not so much a style as a period in history that produced the Second Empire, the Queen Anne, and other late nineteenth century styles, particularly in residential design. Named after Queen Victoria of England (1838 through 1901).

Weathervane. A blade or banner form pivoted on a tower, steeple, or other high point to indicate the direction of the wind.

Bibliography

Ashby, Thompson Eldridge, D.D. *History of the First Parish Church in Brunswick, Maine.* J. French and Son, 1969.

Benes, Philip and Zimmerman, Philip D. *New England Meetinghouse and Church, 1630-1850.* Boston University and The Currier Gallery of Art, 1979.

Bixby, William. *Connecticut, A New Guide.* Charles Scribner's Sons, 1961.

Boston Society of Architects. *Architecture.* Boston. Barre Publishing Co., 1976.

Brown, Elizabeth Mills. *New Haven, A Guide.* Yale University Press, 1976.

Burchard, John and Bush-Brown, Albert. *The Architecture of America.* Little Brown and Company, 1961.

Fleming, John; Honor, Hugh; and Pevsner, Nicholas. *The Penguin Dictionary of Architecture.* Penguin Books, 1966.

Fletcher, Sir Banister. *A History of Architecture on the Comparative Method.* Charles Scribner's Sons, 1961.

Gowans, Alan. *Images of American Living.* J. B. Lippincott, 1964.

Hammett, Ralph W. *Architecture in the United States.* John Wiley and Sons, 1976.

Historic American Buildings Survey. *Maine Catalog.* Maine State Museum, 1974.

Kelly, J. Frederick. *Early Connecticut Meetinghouses.* Columbia University Press, 1948.

Mazmanian, Arthur. *The Structure of Praise.* Beacon Press, 1970.

Pierson, William H., Jr. *American Buildings and Their Architects, Volume I.* Anchor Books, 1976.

Pierson, William H., Jr. *American Buildings and Their Architects, Volume II.* Doubleday & Company, 1978.

Saylor, Henry H. *Dictionary of Architecture.* John Wiley and Sons, 1952.

Sinnott, W. Edmund. *Meetinghouse and Church in Early New England.* McGraw-Hill, 1963.

Stoddard, Whitney S. *Monastery and Cathedral in France.* Wesleyan University Press, 1966.

Whiffen, Marcus. *American Architecture Since 1780.* MIT Press, 1969.

Dictionary References for Glossary

American Heritage Dictionary. 1969, American Heritage and Houghton Mifflin Company.

Oxford Universal Dictionary. 1955, Clarendon Press.

Random House Dictionary. 1966.

Petit Larousse. 1966, Librarie Larousse.

Index

Credits